QUÉBEC

An Illustrated Tour
of 80 Scenic Sites

QUÉBEC
An Illustrated Tour
of 80 Scenic Sites

Published by The Reader's Digest Association (Canada) Ltd, Montréal.

Editor: Ian F. Walker
Art Director: Val Mitrofanow

Design: Andrée Payette
Photo Research: Michelle Turbide
Editorial Assistance: Phyllis Cockfield
Coordination: Susan Wong
Production: Holger Lorenzen

The publisher acknowledges the major contribution of
photographers Mia and Klaus.

The publisher also acknowledges the contributions of
Lyn Martin, Isobel Reid, and John Williams
(Translation and Writing); of Billy Wisse (Proofreading);
and of Gilbert Grand (Index).

Québec: An Illustrated Tour of 80 Scenic Sites is an adaptation
of the Reader's Digest French-language publication
Le Tour du Québec en 80 sites. Editor: Georges Vigny;
Contributing Writer: Jacques Coulon

FIRST EDITION

ISBN: 0-88850-124-2

84 85 86 / 5 4 3 2 1

Printed in Canada

Since 1534, when Jacques Cartier first sailed up the broad blue St. Lawrence, Québec has established itself as a culture distinctively French, a community tempering the traditions of Old France with a New-World spirit of adventure that still runs strong.

Today Canada's biggest province spans an area of 1,540,680 square kilometres and embraces a population of some 6,358,000 people. It is a realm of rural charm, of quaint houses and venerable churches. But it is also a place vibrantly modern, a place unique.

We have tried to capture this uniqueness in *Québec: An Illustrated Tour of 80 Scenic Sites.* And we believe

Introduction

we have succeeded. For if the old saying is true—that a
picture is worth a thousand words—then we have
brought you, our reader, a world that virtually speaks
for itself. Through the eloquent photography of Mia
and Klaus and the splendid talents of almost a dozen
other artists in the field, this book gently illuminates
the elusive essence that is Québec. It portrays the
province in all its glorious seasons, and in all weather.
Here are its snowy capes and sunny beaches, its lush
spring meadows and shining fall foliage.

But we have reached even deeper. *Québec: An
Illustrated Tour of 80 Scenic Sites* sets foot on the

beaches of Tadoussac, where Cartier himself walked
450 years ago. It alights on the windswept shores of
the Magdalens, island home of mariners and fisherfolk.
It pauses momentarily in the verdant farmlands of the
Richelieu River Valley. It watches the sun rise over
the sleeping city of Montréal. It relaxes beside a
tranquil millpond just outside Hull. It celebrates a
fishing festival at La Pérade, a winter carnival at
Chicoutimi, a summer bread-bake at Cookshire. It
savors the sights and smells of a busy open-air market,
the quiet magnificence of a hallowed church, the
simple poetry of an out-of-the-way fishing village. . . .

These, and a medley of other fascinating places, await you in *Québec: An Illustrated Tour of 80 Scenic Sites,* your armchair ticket to discovery. Accompanying each of the featured sites is a brief vignette, a description of things to see and do—and things to know about the place you are visiting: its history, its culture, its eccentricities. Whether you use this book to plan a vacation, to take along with you on a trip, or simply to whet your imagination, we welcome you to the special magic of *La Belle Province.*

The Editors

TO THE READER

The map of Québec locates the 14 regions and 80 sites described in this book. The pages introducing the regions display a smaller version of this map. A stylized regional map, reproduced on each of the site pages, highlights the general location of each of the featured places.

A note on style: Place names and proper names in this book are, for the most part, rendered in French, the preferred practice in Québec today. In a few instances, however, where it was felt that a locale, landmark, or geographical feature was sufficiently well known by its English equivalent, the name was given in that language. Readers interested in learning the meaning of some of the French names in this book will find a helpful glossary on page 204.

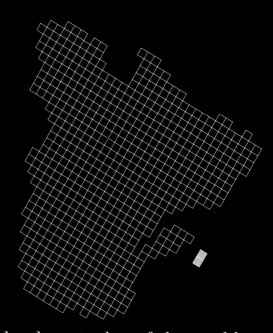

There is a stark, almost edge-of-the-world quality to the Magdalens—and it is this that captures the imaginations of most visitors to these windswept shores. Serviced by regular flights from the mainland (the "continent," as islanders call it) the Magdalens lie in the Gulf of St. Lawrence, some 290 kilometres east of Gaspé. There are about a dozen islands in all, each linked by a narrow stretch of sand which even the roads have difficulty crossing.

Tough, remote, and stormy—yet the landscape is a surprise of colors. Red-hued cliffs compete with pink sand dunes. Casually wooded hillsides contrast with the moody, green sea. Postage-stamp gardens, surrounded by low wooden fences, reflect the changes in the seasons. Even the houses themselves, brightly painted and oddly positioned because of the constant winds, bring a colorful vitality to this hardy land of mariners and fisherfolk—a world at the end of the world, anchored in the wind.

The Magdalen Islands

THE MAGDALEN ISLANDS

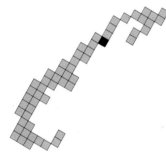

LES SILLONS

Size means little (*above*). The wind always finds a loophole—a brisk reminder of the precarious existence of the fisherfolk who cling to the archipelago's shores.

Chiseled by wind and sculpted by waves, the craggy countenance of an ancient rock (*right*). Despite the sheltering sandbanks, the coastline of Les Sillons testifies to the power of the elements.

Toward the interior of the island of Havre-aux-Maisons, the gently undulating texture of the land becomes increasingly accentuated by low buttes and small valleys which open into lagoons and bays. Locals call these buttes *pelées,* which translates roughly as "baldies." Their meager pasturage is stitched together by straggly bands of spruce and hammered incessantly by the wind.

From the summit of any one of these buttes—they are seldom more than 100 metres or so high—the view stretches as far as South Dune, a gilded arc of sand curving off toward the horizon. Closer by, between the buttes and the seashore, lies Les Sillons, an area of haphazardly scattered houses and fascinatingly contoured sandbanks.

Strong winds and a variety of deposits washed ashore here at high tide have gradually allowed the beach to gain on the sea. This slow advance of land has assumed the form of low ridges, separated from each other by deep furrows, or *sillons.* At a distance, the pinkish sand looks as though a gigantic rake has been dragged across it. The furrows guard the dunes and the vast tidal pools, and are shifted constantly by powerful gales and heavy rains.

On this delicate and wet terrain, a short, coarse form of marram grass manages to survive. Islanders refer to it as "sea hay." These deep-rooting plants have proven impervious to frost and storm, and indispensable in preserving the dunes that lie inland. Their far-reaching tendrils help stabilize the sandbanks, protecting the coastline from the constant assaults of nature.

Along a Shifting Shoreline

THE MAGDALEN ISLANDS

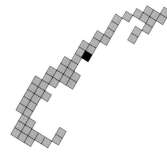

HAVRE-AUX-MAISONS

Space—in this instance, two hillsides for a breakfast view, and the sea not far off—is common currency in the Magdalens (*right*). Indeed, the entire 100-kilometre-long chain is home to fewer than 15,000 people.

Havre-aux-Maisons is an island-village—a reddish, sandy islet awash in the vast Gulf of St. Lawrence. Jacques Cartier was probably the first to anchor off these remote shores, back in 1534. He planted a cross on one of the area's outer islands and named the place Brion, after the French admiral who supported the adventurer's taste for discovery.

Today some 2,000 people live on Havre-aux-Maisons, exacting a simple but hardscrabble existence from soil and sea. Progress, as on all of the Magdalens, came slowly to this place. Even as recently as the late 1940s there were islanders who had never seen trains or street lights or beauty parlors. Modernity has since caught up—but tradition still clings fondly to this island community.

Flat, treeless, and pummeled continuously by winds from the west, Havre-aux-Maisons is by no means the most fertile island in the Magdalen chain. But its ragged coastline is spectacular—with sea-carved notches and strangely eroded red sandstone bluffs. At the rounded Butte, near a series of low-lying cliffs, weird and colorful gypsum formations brighten the landscape. Not far from here, Hydro-Québec has erected an experimental electrical station, powered by a windmill.

At one end, Havre-aux-Maisons is linked to Cap-aux-Meules by a massive sandbank, along which a road runs. At the other end, the island narrows into an area called South Dune, another sandbank, which has pristine beaches and an abundance of seaweed for islanders to harvest in autumn.

The curving arms of these sandbanks—"ribbons," as locals term them—form natural lagoons with narrow openings to the sea, a welcome shelter for fishing boats. The deepest lagoons are on Havre-aux-Maisons and Grande Entrée.

Playground of the Elements

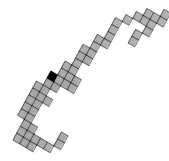

LES CAPS

Coastal dwellers call this unusual landmark "Pointe Hérissée" (*above*). A loose translation would render it as "Bristling Point." Trees atop this rocky pedestal provide the "bristles."

Dangling stakes where the land has fallen away (*right*), and telltale evidence of the erosive power of wind and wave.

Perhaps nowhere in the entire Magdalen Island archipelago is the rugged beauty of this region more evident than at Les Caps, a wave-battered section of headland on the stormy western shore of Ile du Cap-aux-Meules.

For most visitors, Les Caps creates a first impression of wild, unruly grandeur, of multicolored rocks and fantastically eroded cliff bases. In places, enormous overhangs balance precariously on top of concave foundations. Harsh northerlies and mighty blasts from the west have toppled many of these red, gray and yellow sandstone bluffs and sculpted others into strangely shaped pillars, ledges and chasms. What remains is a scenic triumph of nature, a breathtaking masterpiece created by time and the elements.

To reach Les Caps, passengers departing the ferry at Cap-aux-Meules (the town) can drive either north toward Fatima, with its windy grottos and shingly beaches, or south toward the tiny settlement of L'Etang-du-Nord. Regardless of the choice of route, the scenery is equally enticing: churning sea and wheeling seagulls, bobbing fishing boats and abandoned lobster traps, jauntily painted houses and somber herring-smoking shacks.

The full journey around the island takes less than an hour. But a recommended stopping-off point—en route to, or returning from, Les Caps—is the shoreline surrounding Gros-Cap, on the southeastern tip of the island. Here, beside a flashing beacon, a weathered clifftop projects far into the ocean. The view—although strikingly different from that at Les Caps—is exceptional.

A Masterpiece of Nature

THE MAGDALEN ISLANDS

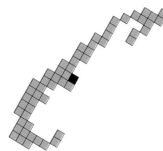

CAP-AUX-MEULES

The "Montréal" of the Magdalens (*above*)—a place of commerce and activity, despite the small-town setting. In the background, the low hills known locally as *demoiselles*.

Floats, boat, and dory (*right*): a typical Magdalen image, and poetry for a visiting camera. Most fishermen in this area sell their catch through local cooperatives.

Its deepwater harbor and central location on the Magdalen island chain make Cap-aux-Meules the archipelago's administrative and commercial hub. Although not the most populated of the islands, Cap-aux-Meules blossoms with tourists throughout summer. The town is well serviced by an airport, a hospital, a good selection of shops, restaurants and motels, and a busy pier (where ever-present trawlers and merchant ships anchor). From the pier, the Prince Edward Island ferry comes and goes regularly.

Cap-aux-Meules is endowed with a sparse, remote kind of beauty. The terrain is flat, except for an occasional low hill rising out of the reddish soil. Magdalen Islanders call these hills *demoiselles* (spinsters). Treeless, and rounded by relentless winds, they contain just enough vegetation for a handful of determined farmers to eke out a living. Most of these solitary hills have been affectionately nicknamed by local inhabitants, as have a number of other physical characteristics that distinguish this otherwise uniform land: sea-scarred peaks, sandy coves and weird rock formations.

While farming is less than lucrative, fishing—as on most of the islands—is a staple source of income. (Indeed, each year this skinny little archipelago lands more than one quarter of all the fish caught in Québec.) Lobsters from Cap-aux-Meules are particularly prized. To ensure freshness, the lobsters are kept alive in fish wells until they are ready to be shipped to the mainland.

One of the island's principal attractions is a hike along the Chemin des Caps, from which a magnificent panorama of landscape and seascape unfolds. Other highlights include the artisans' cooperative, the herring smokehouses and some of the islands' most beautiful homes, built in the traditional Madelinot style.

Crossroads of the Magdalens

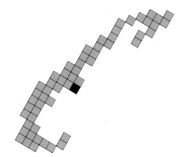

GROS-CAP

A typical Gros-Cap dwelling (*above*). The muster of colors—red chimney, blue wall, and white trim—manage to add cheer to a brooding, if captivating, landscape.

Contented sheep and a weathered barn (*right*)—but something less than a farm. Harsh weather and poor soil in this area conspire against anyone attempting to work the land.

Remote and enchanting, the tiny village of Gros-Cap overlooks a lonely stretch of sandy beach that curves around the Baie de Plaisance. Located some five kilometres south of the town of Cap-aux-Meules, it nestles between the little harbor of La Martinique and the rocky spur of Cap-Rouge.

The landscape surrounding Gros-Cap is informed by low-lying cliffs—some no higher than 12 metres—and numerous miniscule bays and ponds. Broad bands of sand entwine these scoops of water, separating them from the sea. Slow erosion has transformed some of the ponds into marshy areas tufted with thin, short blades of grass. North of the village, the terrain gives way to gentle dales that sweep gradually upward, reaching as high as the Butte, which is situated near the center of the island.

Deep-sea fishing is not as common now in these parts as it was in the past; the sea's yield—in this particular region—was simply not lucrative enough to support the local population. And the land itself was never very suitable for farming. Consequently, many inhabitants have moved on to more favorable climes. Most of those who stay on are employed by the lobster cannery or the nearby shipbuilding yard, which manufactures small craft. Both of these industries are at Pointe-de-l'Echouerie.

During summer, this corner of the Magdalen archipelago becomes a popular camping spot, with its promise of peaceful isolation. It is indeed a study in solitude, seductive in its desolateness.

A Study in Solitude

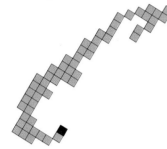

THE MAGDALEN ISLANDS

HAVRE-AUBERT

At Havre-Aubert (*above*), fishing is first and foremost. A host of local canneries, freezing plants, and smokehouses await the next catch.

Rest from a busy season (*right*). Houses on hilltops, boats warming in the sun—a lifestyle governed by the rhythms and moods of the sea.

The tiny port of Havre-Aubert nestles on an island—also called Havre-Aubert—at the southeastern tip of the Magdalen archipelago. Situated in an isolated cove, the village looks onto a long fishhook of sand and rock which curves out into the vast Atlantic. This narrow promontory—known as Sandy Hook—shelters the weathered port from the seasonal furies of wind and sea.

From April to November, fishing is Havre-Aubert's principal activity. Boats come and go continually, laden with herring, mackerel, smelt, lobster and other shellfish. During the summer months visitors too can savor the tang of open sea, on organized fishing expeditions.

As in many of the hamlets along the Baie de Plaisance, the brightly painted cottages of Havre-Aubert originally belonged to Acadian settlers fleeing Nova Scotia in the 1750s. The settlers brought little baggage but an enduring sense of religion. The modern-style church in the village is an elegant reminder of this fact.

A high grassy knoll to the west of the village gives an excellent prospect of the entire island, its magnificent sandy beaches and red sandstone cliffs. Nearby, on a large headland dominating the road, a stately white building houses the Marine Museum. The museum focuses on the Madelinots' daily life and their close ties with the sea. There is an informative display of fishing methods and types of boats, some re-created in miniature. Fragments and objects washed ashore from local shipwrecks are also exhibited.

A 'Hook' to Catch the Wind

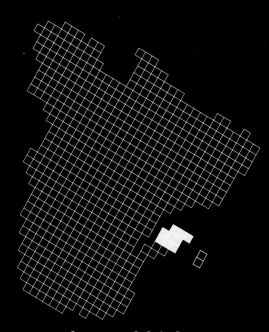

Some 850 kilometres of coastal highway weaves through the Gaspé peninsula, opening up a world of striking scenic diversity. Sharply contoured cliffs tinted red and gray overlook broad beaches. Farther inland the rugged, river-creased landscape gives way to the Chic-Chocs, Eastern Canada's highest mountains. Some of the Gaspé's most scenic landmarks cluster at the tip of the peninsula: Forillon National Park, the Baie de Gaspé, Rocher-Percé, and Ile de Bonaventure.

All along the Gaspé perimeter, tiny colorful fishing villages dot the landscape. Patches of rich green forest here have been cleared for farmland, and miniature fishing fleets moor against aging piers. Despite 30 years of struggle to overcome chronic underdevelopment, the Gaspé is just as it always has been—quiet, easygoing, a visitor's delight.

The Gaspé

THE GASPÉ

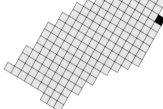

ILE DE BONAVENTURE

Spring through fall is the time to visit (*above*). Throughout these seasons garrulous gulls await, as do exotic arctic puffins. In summer, boats leave on the hour.

Layer upon layer (*right*), each nook and cranny bustles with birds. The island is a five-kilometre ride by boat from the beaches of Percé.

Jacques Cartier anchored at Ile de Bonaventure in 1534 and named it in celebration of his voyage across the Atlantic. But it was not until about 1800 that the first settlers—the Janvrin and Le Boutillier brothers—arrived. Along with 40 other families, they established a community and made a living off the rich local fishing grounds. Over the years, however, the settlement died off, and today no one lives on the island. It is home, instead, to a magnificent colony of seabirds.

Lying just offshore from Percé, tiny Ile de Bonaventure is no more than a few square kilometres in area. In 1971 the entire island became the property of the Department of Tourism, Games and Fisheries. Three years later it was designated a refuge for migratory birds.

With a population of more than 50,000 gannets, Ile de Bonaventure is one of the largest gull sanctuaries in the world. Cormorants, kittiwakes, and razor-billed auks are among the other species that jostle with the gannets for space along the beaches and sheltered outcroppings. They arrive in mid-April and certain species remain until the end of November.

Tour boats from the wharf at Percé carry visitors to the island. As a boat draws near, great ledges swarming with gannets come into view, giving sightseers a close-range glimpse of the birds' activities.

Tour guides conduct short walks along four hiking trails which ramble over the island and through a small evergreen forest carpeted with moss, lichens, and mushrooms. Visitors are free to walk among the flocks of birds. So at ease are the gulls with their human guests that they will remain calmly perched for close-up photographs.

A Family of 50,000, More or Less

THE GASPÉ

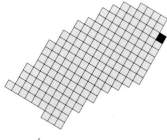

PERCÉ

A one-legged figurehead and what else? Percé (*above*)—a village of surprises and shipshape customs, a village dedicated to the sea. In its time it was the largest fishing center in the Gaspé.

Early-morning mist (*right*) spreads a veil across the sleeping village of Percé. Even the gulls of nearby Rocher-Percé are unlikely to waken the residents; the cry of birds here is as unnoticed as the wash of the sea.

Giant and shiplike (*pages 32, 33*): a rock beached for eternity, its hull pierced by the sea. Even in the time of Champlain—who named it in 1534—the rock had its now-famous arch.

Route 132 climbs to the foot of Pic de l'Aurore past rocky outcroppings and long, quiet beaches on Coin-du-Banc—then descends gradually toward the coastline. Near the crest of this highway visitors come face to face with their first view of Percé and its surrounding seascape: a breathtaking panorama of village, cape, jutting rock, and somber silhouette of Ile de Bonaventure. No photographer, even on a clear day, can truly capture this area's rugged splendor.

Rooted in a small bay since time immemorial, Percé's famous rock is composed of layered limestone sediments embedded with millions of fossils. Relentless winds and tides have crafted a gigantic arch into its side. Originally the rock was triple-arched and formed part of a huge mountainous structure attached to Mont-Joli. Since then its bulk has diminished. Today it stands 88 metres high and 433 metres long, its base dappled with seaweed and splashed by gulf sprays, its flanks alive with flocks of screaming seabirds from early spring to mid-autumn.

Throughout summer, these craggy, scenic shores draw hordes of visitors—to saunter along untamed beaches, explore hidden coves, do a little sea fishing, chat with waterfront locals, or simply take in the sounds, smells and colors of the ever-busy harbor. At low tide Rocher-Percé is accessible by foot and becomes a treasure-trove of delightful aquatic souvenirs. Starfish, mussels, and sea urchins carpet the sea-path, and visitors who are lucky and sharp-eyed can occasionally discover a few brightly banded agates nestled in the sand.

Brooding Rock and Ageless Arch

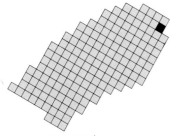

BAIE DE GASPÉ

Old man and the sea—an epic that began long before Hemingway, perhaps even before the time of Cartier's landing here (*above*). Fishing is still the dominant occupation in this region.

The play of light and bay (*right*). A single glance can scarcely take in the immensity of the Baie de Gaspé. Even with a population of thousands, much of the area remains sparsely settled.

Highway 132 skirts Forillon National Park, slips past Cap-des-Rosiers, then curves toward the right at a breathtaking angle. From here, the wild, unruly splendor of the Gaspé unfolds in one vast sweep as the road dips toward Cap-aux-Os and the Baie de Gaspé. Visitors enjoying this view can readily grasp why the original Indian inhabitants named this region *Gaspeg*—"the place where the land ends."

Stretching out toward the horizon lies the lovely Baie de Gaspé, a 30-kilometre-long finger of water opening into the Atlantic. The bay is actually a large natural harbor, sheltered from seasonal storms by Cap Bon-Ami, a towering limestone promontory at the tip of the Gaspé Peninsula. The town of Gaspé, a busy fishing port at the mouth of the York River, hugs the south side of the bay.

Although situated a thousand kilometres from Montréal—at the "end of the railway line," as locals like to say—Gaspé has a population of almost 17,000. Many of these residents make their living from the sea. Canada's oldest fish hatchery, established here in 1876, processes as many as a million salmon and trout fry annually.

Jacques Cartier landed in this area on July 24, 1534, claiming it in the name of France, and erecting a cross to mark the event. The town raised a nine-metre granite cross here 400 years later, to commemorate the original wooden one.

Visitors can learn more of the history of this region at the Gaspé Museum, with its exhibits relating to Cartier and even to the time of the Vikings.

A Shining Bay at Land's End

THE GASPÉ

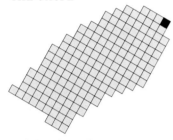

PIC DE L'AURORE

A cascade of fog rolling in from the sea, gently probing the slopes of Pic de l'Aurore (*right*). Air and light here are said to be purer than elsewhere.

Sunlight affects its moods, and the sea complements them. Yet at any hour of the day Pic de l'Aurore (or Dawn Peak, as it is sometimes called) is a sight to behold. Towering more than 180 metres above the Gulf of St. Lawrence, this majestic cliff wall stands almost midway between L'Anse-au-Beaufils, in the south, and the town of Percé, in the north.

A crest of soft, short grass caps this magnificent peak. When rippled by the wind, the grass reflects the patterns of light in the sky. Sunrise paints the cliffside pink. At other times of day the peak takes on various hues of purple and gold.

A hiking trail connects Pic de l'Aurore with the town of Percé. The trail passes by way of Mont Ste-Anne, where the view embraces Rocher-Percé, Ile de Bonaventure, and the vast Baie des Chaleurs.

Depending on the direction from which one approaches it, Pic de l'Aurore yields strikingly different profiles. From the south, the terrain rises gradually toward the summit, revealing a vista of sheer cliff and open sea. From the north, the peak's ocher face comes into full view. Strewn along the beach below are chunks of rock, massive in themselves, that have broken away from the enormous wall.

The history of this famous Gaspesian landmark dates back many millennia, to a time when tremendous geological forces pushed, folded, and squeezed the region's limestone and shale formations into a multitude of irregular configurations. The coastline in this area still bears the scars of that upheaval, with its many cliffs and small mountains, and an untold number of crevices and valleys.

A Peak Crowned by Light

THE GASPÉ

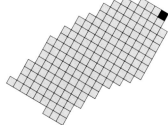

CAP-DES-ROSIERS

An armada of ice floes salutes Cap-des-Rosiers (*above*). It was from these shores that villagers first spied the British invading fleet of 1759, bound for Québec City and a historic outcome.

Set in the cold night, the Cap-des-Rosiers lighthouse (*right*) looks out on perilous waters where many a ship was wrecked.

Cap-des-Rosiers, a majestic cape named by Champlain for its lively profusion of wild roses, stands at the tip of the Gaspé Peninsula, where the St. Lawrence flows into the Gulf and where Route 132 enters Forillon National Park. Near the foot of the cape lies an old fishing village of the same name.

Sadly, the rose bushes have all but vanished from the cape. But in every direction the surrounding landscape provides changing—and equally enchanting—vistas. Flanked by hidden coves and sheer headlands, the white cottages of Cap-des-Rosiers occupy a level plateau not far above the water. Low flatlands at the base of the cliffs have become a patchwork of carefully tended fields. Nearby, the rambling, forested coastline opens dramatically onto the sea.

The waters around Cap-des-Rosiers were favored by mariners as far back as the 1500s, when fishermen spread their codfish out to dry on the huge smooth rocks that line the shore. In recent decades, however, fishing has diminished as a source of livelihood in this area. Many inhabitants have moved elsewhere; a few farmers have clung to the land.

Fishermen and sailors have always accorded this wild and treacherous stretch of coastline a healthy respect, for it has been the site of many tragic shipwrecks. Among the most famous of these was the *Garricks*, which went down in 1847, crowded with Irish immigrants. In the wake of the disaster, the Cap-des-Rosiers lighthouse was begun. The lighthouse stands today as a reminder of that grim sea-faring era, and as a guide to modern-day ships plying these ancient waters. At 33 metres, it is the tallest such structure in the region.

Yesteryear's Roses Remembered

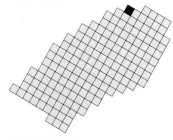

MADELEINE

A spacious, circular shore (*above*) separates the twin settlements of Rivière-la-Madeleine and Madeleine-Centre. As if to confuse matters further, the communities lie near the mouth of a similarly named river—Rivière Madeleine.

A monochrome of winter (*right*). Lonely at any time of year, Madeleine endures as a symbol of Gaspesian hardiness. Here: the rugged and irregular coastline that confronted the earliest settlers.

From Anse-Pleureuse to Rivière-la-Madeleine, the northeast coast of the Gaspé becomes at once unpredictable and fascinating—a mix of towering limestone cliffs, shingly beaches, jutting headlands, and forested mountainsides which plunge suddenly into cultivated lowlands. Around the mouth of the Rivière Madeleine, the shore widens and the coastline forms a vast arc. A long ribbon of white sand in the center of the river delta serves as a dividing line between the twin villages of Madeleine-Centre, to the west, and Rivière-la-Madeleine, to the east.

Although both villages are typically Gaspesian, visitors will notice subtle differences between the two. Rivière-la-Madeleine's cottages are scattered throughout deep coves, grassy headlands, and sandy strands along the riverbank. At Madeleine-Centre the dominating feature is an old, silver-steepled church, surrounded by a number of clapboard dwellings. Close-by, on a bald promontory overlooking the St. Lawrence, a round-towered lighthouse, one of the oldest in the region, stands out against the sky.

The location of both communities—near an estuary—reflects a time when there was neither road nor railway here; the river was the only way into the peninsula's interior. (Many old Gaspé settlements are similarly located.) Today, in spite of Highway 132, the sense of remoteness prevails.

Settlement came slowly to this area, principally in the 1850s, and for many decades the main source of income was cod-fishing. A pulp-and-paper industry flared briefly into being, but the economic collapse of 1929 extinguished this financial promise. Nowadays the 900 inhabitants of both villages have returned to fishing, farming, and—to a lesser extent—forestry for their livelihoods.

In the Heart of the Gaspé

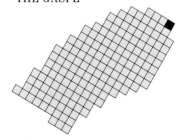

FORILLON NATIONAL PARK

Contrasts unite in the splendor of this region (*above*). Forillon knits together coves and beaches—and dense forest that ends abruptly at the sea.

Exotic as Bermuda, fresh as an English countryside (*right*)— this is Forillon at its best. Waterfall and footpath, a wealth of nature for the asking.

Forillon National Park lies at the northeastern tip of the Gaspé Peninsula. Established in 1971 with "harmony between man, land, and sea" for its official theme, it is one of Canada's newest national parks—a jagged, sea-washed expanse of limestone cliffs and fir-clad highlands overlooking the gentle Baie de Gaspé.

Three spacious campgrounds and several picnic areas and hiking trails make the park a magnet for summertime tourists. But countless sandy coves, hidden along the peninsula's ragged shoreline, provide seclusion aplenty. At the park entrance, a visitor information center details the area's many attractions. In the evenings, there are slide shows and lectures.

Wildlife in the park is abundant. The cliffs are a haven for seabirds: herring gulls, black guillemots, double-crested cormorants, and many varieties of ducks are among the 150 bird species that make their home here. White-tailed deer, moose, beaver, otter, lynx, mink, muskrat, red fox and weasel—and a host of other mammals—also inhabit the park. Offshore, whales and seals are regular summer visitors.

The name Forillon has been used here since the days of New France. One explanation is that it derives from *pharillon*, meaning "little lighthouse," and that the first *pharillon* was a rock on which fires were lit to guide fishermen to good beaches during the 17th century. The rock—which lay off Cap de Gaspé, at the extreme tip of the peninsula—has long since crumbled into the sea. But the good beaches remain, as do the rich fishing bounties of mackerel and herring that attracted those mariners of old.

Man, Land, and Sea 'in Harmony'

THE GASPÉ

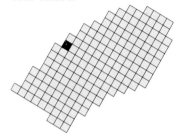

STE-ANNE-DES-MONTS

A place of worship at the threshold of a coveted wilderness (*right*). Resting along the rocky shore of a bay, the spot was named by Champlain in honor of Pierre de Monts, first governor of Acadia (1604).

Perched on the craggy north shore of the Gaspé peninsula, Ste-Anne-des-Monts is the largest town between Matane and Gaspé. It lies 500 kilometres east of Québec City, near the mouth of the Rivière Ste-Anne. The population of approximately 7,000 depends for its livelihood on farming, cod-fishing, lumbering and tourism.

Probably the most popular tourist attraction is the imposing granite church overlooking the St. Lawrence, to which thousands of worshipers pilgrimage annually. Dedicated to Saint Anne, patron of sailors, the shrine holds what is said to be a fragment of bone from the saint's finger.

The town itself stands at the busy intersection of highways 132 (the coastal route) and 299 (which crosses the peninsula, linking up with the prosperous fishing communities of Baie des Chaleurs). This easily accessible location has made the place both the commercial and educational center for this part of the Gaspé.

To Quebeckers familiar with the area, Ste-Anne is the gateway to wilderness vacations. Just south of town, on Highway 299, lies the spectacular Parc de la Gaspésie—one of the region's most favored tourist destinations. This rugged expanse of parkland contains a dense network of rivers and streams where anglers can fish for trout and tasty ouananiche (landlocked salmon). Visitors can wander some 240 kilometres of hiking trails, picnic at several lovely sites, and enjoy the crystalline waters of Lac Madeleine. Guides will take climbers to Mont Jacques-Cartier's 1268-metre summit—the highest in the Chic-Chocs. Here, on the airy mountain slopes, moose and deer roam free, as does one of the world's last herds of woodland caribou.

A Gateway to the Wilderness

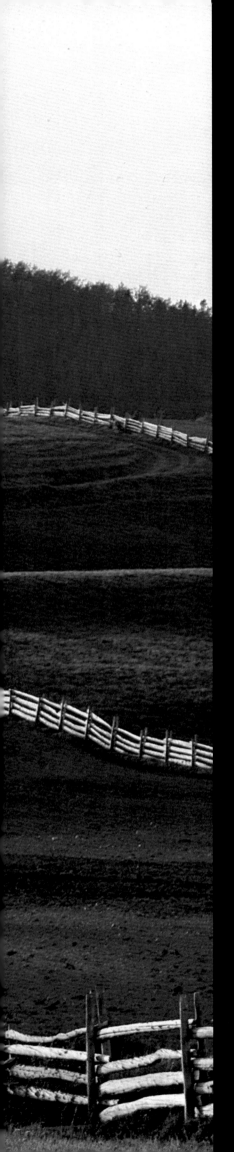

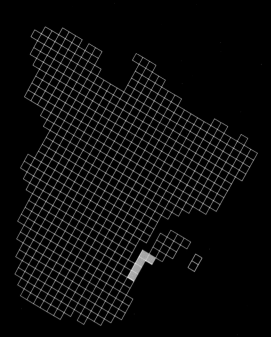

Ask a Quebecker about the location of the lower St. Lawrence region, and he will probably be pressed for an answer—short of suggesting that it lies along the south shore, somewhere between Québec City and Gaspé. More precisely defined, however, the Lower St. Lawrence runs from La Pocatière to Ste-Luce-sur-Mer, a distance of some 200 kilometres, and is made up of four municipal counties—Kamouraska, Rivière-du-Loup, Témiscouata, and Rimouski. The entire region embraces a population of slightly more than 125,000.

Despite the seeming vagueness of its geography, the world of the Lower St. Lawrence is eminently real. It is a realm of fishing boats and farmyards where the tang of salt water often mingles with the smell of freshly worked fields and deep, pungent forests. Sandy beaches line many of the region's bays and coves, and a number of the islands here are host to myriad seabirds and shorebirds. Industry consists primarily of forestry and tourism.

The Lower St. Lawrence

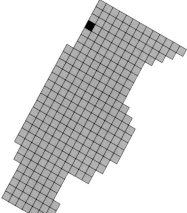

RIMOUSKI

Rimouski (*above*), and the St. Lawrence beyond: a city of old churches, modern office buildings, and superb art galleries.

Stripped fields are a common sight along the road to Rimouski (*right*). Peat moss is cultivated for eventual sale in landscaping nurseries throughout the region.

Old and new live side by side in Rimouski, a bustling port city near the mouth of the St. Lawrence, some 300 kilometres east of Québec City. With the river at its doorstep and fertile plains for a backyard, the city stands on the site of one of the first seigneuries in this region. Buildings from the area's history include the cathedral of St-Germain-de-Rimouski (1854) and the Rimouski Regional Museum, originally a church (1823). Some of Québec's finest art treasures, ranging from the works of Suzor-Coté to those of Charles Huot, brighten the airy interior of this superb museum.

Although the past is cherished in Rimouski, many of its buildings are both modern and commercial, and less than a quarter of a century old. Set amid inviting parks and green spaces, they rise clean and phoenix-like on the remains of a disastrous fire that leveled almost one third of the city in a single night in 1950.

Today, with a population of 40,000, the "new" Rimouski has the distinction of being the educational heart of the Lower St. Lawrence. A branch of the Université du Québec is located here, as are the Institut de marine du Québec, the National Institute for Scientific and Oceanographic Research, and the Pointe-au-Père Aquaculture Center.

Not all, however, is academia. In August a five-day farm fair annually attracts more than 20,000 people. The Rimouski Fall Festival in late October features pheasant hunting, smelt fishing, shooting contests and exhibitions.

On the Doorstep of the Gulf

THE LOWER ST. LAWRENCE

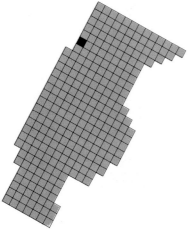

BIC

An intimate meeting of water and hills (*above*). Sea otters and harbor and harp seals frequently visit the reefs and rocky shores of the Bic area.

Afternoon shadows parade across the fields of Bic (*right*), an area that artists, vacationers, and nature lovers all cherish.

From the cliff overlooking the village of Bic and the island-dotted St. Lawrence, it is easy to grasp why this strategic location inspired ambitious schemes. Count Frontenac, governor of New France, wanted to build a naval base here. His dream was never realized. Neither was the plan to make Bic the biggest merchant port downstream from Québec City—even though a proliferation of fishermen and sailors in these parts ensured a supply of skilled labor. Despite its apparent commercial potential, Bic has never become more than a desirable vacation spot, a place of idyllic tranquility especially favored by writers and nature lovers.

At low tide, most of the nearby islands can be reached on foot from Bic. Ile du Bic, the largest of the chain, was a popular stopping-off point for fishing boats and schooners traveling along the river. Today, vacationers come for deep-sea fishing, for camping, or simply to stroll past the sandbanks and marshes frequented by thousands of seabirds and shorebirds. A number of popular hiking trails wind up to the Mont St-Louis lookout. From there, on a clear day, visitors can view the distant north shore of the St. Lawrence, almost 40 kilometres away.

The village itself has a population of about 3,000. Although it contains several old buildings, its true treasures are a covered bridge and two flour mills, all dating to the last century. One of the mills, the Lavoie, still maintains an impressive wooden overshot wheel in working condition.

A Favorite Beauty Spot

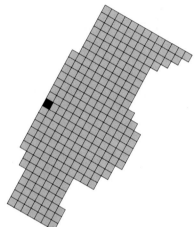

ISLE-VERTE

This method of fishing (*right*)—common in the Isle-Verte area—is called *pêche à fascines*. Nets are hoisted on poles at low tide, and high tide brings in the catch. At times, however, the harvest is little more than foamy waves dispatched by a capricious river.

The highway west from Cacouna veers abruptly from the rocky shores of the St. Lawrence and heads inland for almost 15 kilometres through a varied landscape of fertile plains, cultivated fields and low, tree-strewn hills. As it rejoins the coast, the road crosses a narrow bridge spanning the Rivière Verte. Beyond the bridge lies the hillside village of Isle-Verte.

With a population of only 1,200, Isle-Verte is one of the smallest communities on the St. Lawrence south shore. Most of its inhabitants make their livings by fishing for eel or herring, or by farming. Visitors can sample the fruits of this lifestyle each August, when the village hosts a large country fair.

A Gothic-style church and a seigneurial mill—both dating to the middle of the last century—are typical examples of traditional regional architecture, and well worth a visit. But the main appeal of Isle-Verte lies just outside the village, at its wildlife park.

This splendid *réserve faunique* is a birdwatcher's delight. Thousands of multicolored seabirds and shorebirds—including gulls, ducks, herons, plovers and cormorants—nest in the small ponds that dot the marshy riverbank and in the nearby fields and irrigation ditches. Herds of seals, too, can often be glimpsed sunning themselves off a short spit of land that juts into the St. Lawrence.

Ile-Verte, the island, is five kilometres offshore. Visitors can arrange transportation to this tiny fishing community (population 200) through local boat owners, for a small fee. A magnificent beach curves around the island's north shore. Nearby stands Québec's oldest operating lighthouse, dating back to 1809.

By Beach and Lighthouse

THE LOWER ST. LAWRENCE

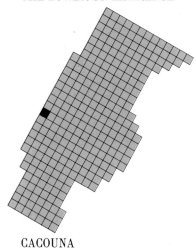

CACOUNA

To eat or not to eat (*above*)—
that seems to be the question,
here in the warm, clear
morning light. Farming has
always been a major element of
life in the Lower St. Lawrence
region, and animal husbandry
has played its part.

Cacouna's short summer throws
light on a modest farmyard
scene (*right*), an image
representative of today, yet
strangely at odds with the well-
heeled lifestyle that
characterized its past. Stables
in those days housed not work
horses but fleet racetrack
thoroughbreds.

Like the neighboring coastal villages of Notre-Dame-du-
Portage, St-Patrice and St-Fabien, St-Georges-de-Cacouna is
considered one of the most pleasing holiday spots on the
south shore of the St. Lawrence. It emerged as a tourist resort
shortly after the first railway arrived in the area, in 1860.

Before the railway, only a handful of settlers—and
occasional *voyageurs*—occupied the area; with improved
transportation, however, wealthy city vacationers traveled
to the place. These visitors built elegant summer villas
along the riverfront, much like those in La Malbaie and Pointe-
au-Pic on the opposite shore. By the early part of this century,
Cacouna already had a luxurious hotel large enough to
accommodate 600 guests.

As members of high society flocked to the town, they
brought with them a taste for horse racing and sumptuous
soirées. Cacouna became compared to the plush New York
resort town of Saratoga Springs—indeed, it was even nicknamed the "Saratoga of Canada." With increased popularity,
however, Cacouna lost much of its exclusiveness and,
gradually, the leisure class migrated to other resort towns,
such as Rivière-du-Loup, 10 kilometres west.

Remnants of Cacouna's gracious past are evident in its
lovely fieldstone church, its Capuchin monastery (once the
summer residence of a shipping merchant) and in the stately
Victorian villas lining the coast.

For motorists traveling west from Cacouna and wishing to
explore the north shore, a ferry at Rivière-du-Loup crosses
regularly to St-Siméon, about 20 kilometres away.

Twilight of a Gilded Past

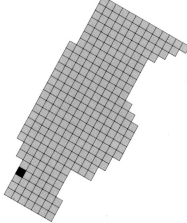

KAMOURASKA

An aging, spacious home in Andréville (*above*), at the edge of Kamouraska County. Note the traditional, slide-like design of the metal-covered roof—an advantage against heavy falls of snow.

The tranquil countryside surrounding Kamouraska (*right*) extends a standing invitation to stop the car, spread out the picnic cloth on the grass, and enjoy the charms of an abundant, rustic landscape.

The Kamouraska region occupies an enchanting realm of green meadows, rich farmlands, and low wooded hills 160 kilometres downriver from Québec City, on the south shore of the St. Lawrence. The village itself, with its narrow streets descending toward the river, is a parade of vintage architecture—the Paradis mill, the Taché manor, the handsome church and vicarage, and the many distinguished century-old residences.

Founded some 300 years ago, the village was once part of a large seigneury embracing 17 parishes and an area of more than 100 square kilometres. Little changed from the past, Kamouraska today is principally a fishing and farming community. Eels, which are shipped to Europe, are a staple source of income. The eels are caught between rows of stakes—called weir traps—which divert the fish into snares where they are eventually netted.

Not far from the village church and the Kamouraska Museum, the schooner *Monica L* lies moored beside an aging wharf. This old vessel is a poignant reminder of a more prosperous time when similar ships transported cargoes of lumber between Québec and Trois-Rivières, docking frequently at Kamouraska.

Facing the river, beside the highway, stands the four-chimneyed Maison L'Anglais, which achieved momentary fame in the film version of Anne Hébert's popular novel, *Kamouraska*. The house dates to 1725.

Beyond the salt marshes of the bay lies a chain of six tiny islands. Craggy ledges and reefs along this miniature archipelago provide a haven for migratory birds. The birds are most plentiful in fall.

Old Ways in a Novel Setting

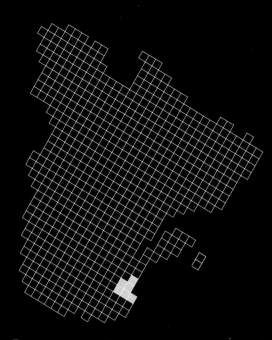

South of the St. Lawrence, from Lotbinière to Montmagny and down along the Chaudière River, the quietly undulating landscape supports more than 4,000 maple groves. September and October paint these green-leafed hillsides with a palette of gentle autumn russets, and the winter months freeze them into Christmas-card stillness. In spring, however, this area—known as "the Beauce"—bustles with activity: Tapped maples drip their sap into metal buckets; sprightly tunes and wisps of smoke curl from the chimneys of sugar shacks among the trees; lovers of maple syrup, maple sugar, and other such Québec springtime delicacies arrive in droves at these *cabanes à sucre*. It is a time of celebration, of songs, toasts, and *joie de vivre*.

Quebeckers are justly proud of their maple forests—and this region has the greatest concentration of maples in the world. There are also more than ten thousand dairy farms scattered throughout the countryside, especially in the Ste-Marie–St-Georges area. Farther east, toward the Maine border, small townships continue to make their living off the forests and farmlands much as in colonial days. From Leclercville to Lévis the St. Lawrence is bordered by old seigneurial villages where grand churches and old manors evoke the spirit of a former time.

Maple Country

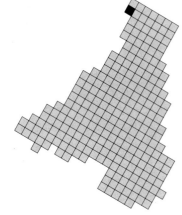

ST-JEAN-PORT-JOLI

Joli—as in St-Jean-Port-Joli—means "pretty" in French. And pretty the town is, with its village simplicity, sunny church spire, and modest cottages (*above*). The parish dates to 1721 but the present stone church was built some six decades later.

A proud boast but true: the French inscription carved into this centuries-old tree (*right*) translates, "Here lies the hand-crafting capital of Québec, in St-Jean-Port-Joli, at the mouth of the Rivière Trois-Saumons."

Three uniquely talented brothers inspired the revival of the traditional Québec craft of wood-carving in St-Jean-Port-Joli. Like their carpenter father before them, Médard, André and Jean-Julien Bourgault were master woodworkers. They opened a wood-carving studio in 1928 and, even during the economically bleak 1930s, discovered that there were travelers eager to buy their handsome figurines. By 1940 the brothers had trained scores of villagers in the craft, and a tradition that had been in decline began once again to flourish.

Today the small south shore village of 3,300 is known as the wood-carving capital of Québec, with some 50 studios displaying carvings of habitants and historical and religious figures, as well as sculpted murals, miniature animals, and tiny sailboats. The reputation of its 200 or so craftsmen extends well beyond the boundaries of Québec—to the rest of Canada, the United States, and even to Europe. Most studios are located in the western half of the village, and along both sides of Route 132.

Intricately carved sculptures also grace many craftsmen's dwellings, including the Médard Bourgault home which stands not far from the village inn. Since Médard's death in 1967, the house has been open to visitors. Although a wealth of exquisite carvings waits within, the sculpted doors and panels of the exterior make the house a work of art in itself. Médard's work also graces the pulpit of the old church (1779), which stands nearby. He fashioned this magnificent sculpture along with his brother Jean-Julien.

Though wood carving dominates this tiny waterfront community, the town also embraces a host of other artistic activities. Locals create beautiful copper-enamel art and jewelry, woven fabrics of striking design, as well as oil paintings, mosaics, and works in leather and metal.

A Colony of Craftsmen

MONTMAGNY

Montmagny, with its river and falls (*above*). One of the highlights of a visit to this town is the 1634 communal mill, powered by wind or water. The ground floor is now a museum displaying mill components.

Spring, a saltwater beach, and a chattering congregation of new arrivals (*right*). Blue-winged teals and white geese frequent these beaches, but the geese dominate. Montmagny skies have filled with as many as 200,000 white geese in a single season.

Come spring and autumn, the skies above Montmagny play host to a spectacular array of migrating birds, as white geese, mallards, and snipes arrive by the tens of thousands. Indeed, so much a part of the local landscape are these birds that Montmagny celebrates their presence with an annual White Goose Festival. The event is held each October.

Founded in 1646, Montmagny has been as much a witness to the passage of history as it has been to the passage of birds. But unless you venture off Highway 132—which cuts right through Montmagny—it is easy to miss the treasures of this small town's past. Several interesting old homes hide their charms along narrow backstreets. Among these is the restored wooden Manoir Couillard-Dupuis (1768), which now serves as a tourist bureau. A large stone bread-oven dominates the ground floor; upstairs, local handicrafts are sold. The 18th-century Taché House—one-time home of Sir Etienne Paschal Taché, a Father of Confederation—is also open to the public. Taché was born and practised medicine here. The nearby Manoir des Erables (1814) is now a cosy inn with an excellent culinary reputation.

From the Montmagny pier, a ferry departs for Ile-aux-Grues and Ile-aux-Oies, both popular bird sanctuaries. These two islands in the middle of the St. Lawrence are encircled by grass-tufted sand dunes and inviting sandy beaches.

Two other small islands slightly farther west are also worth visiting. Grosse Ile was a 19th-century immigrant quarantine station. On Ile aux Basques there are furnaces used by 16th-century Basque fishermen to extract whale oil.

Twice a Year, a Skyful of Birds

MAPLE COUNTRY

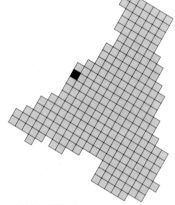

BEAUMONT

More than a century and a half old, Beaumont's lovely mill (*above*) continues to churn out flour, and history. It is one of Québec's lesser-known beauty spots. The essence of antiquity, it straddles the river in a state of almost perfect conservation.

An autumn shade of maple, a quiet mill pond (*right*). Few of us can recall the days when such mills were centerpieces of community life; but we cannot fail to feel a trace of nostalgia at such a sight. Almost dutiful to tradition and sentiment, the Beaumont wheel spins on.

Perched high on the south shore of the St. Lawrence, some 15 kilometres east of Lévis, Beaumont occupies the center of a rich agricultural heartland. This region was dubbed the "Canadian Normandy" by a traveler in the 1920s, and there is a definite resemblance between the landscape of that old French province and the rolling hills of Bellechasse County. Prosperous dairy farms dotted with trees and bordered by hedges are found throughout. There are also numerous ancient houses, as well as a church and presbytery that date to the early 18th century.

Beaumont's most impressive landmark, however, is a 160-year-old flour mill—a *moulin*—atop a cliff overlooking the river. Constructed in the Normandy style typical of much Québec colonial architecture, the structure supports three floors and a granary topped by a mansard roof. Thirty-eight windows furnish light to the interior. The foundations and wheel cage are of masonry.

When the mill was built in 1821, it served as a wool separator. For several years afterward it was owned by a miller's son from St-Charles-de-Bellechasse who used it to grind grain. The mill changed hands several times but continued to be used for the same purpose.

The mill today is fully operational and has been completely restored. It now stands as a cherished monument to yesteryear, a place where visitors can watch the process of grinding and admire artifacts from the past.

A Turning Wheel, A Bygone Era

66

MAPLE COUNTRY

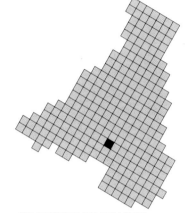

ST-JOSEPH-DE-BEAUCE

Ice clings to the edge of the
road leading to St-Joseph-de-
Beauce (*above*), reluctantly
relinquishing its winter grip on
the town. Spring is a perilous
time of year here, when the
seasonal thaw is apt to cause
the Chaudière to overflow its
banks.

Spring comes to St-Joseph-de-
Beauce (*right*), in the heart of
the recently designated "Maple
Country," a region whose
output of maple syrup and
sugar accounts for more than
half of Québec's total yield. The
photograph shows a traditional
sleigh-mounted barrel making
its rounds, collecting the spring
flow of sap from the maple
trees.

St-Joseph-de-Beauce is a flourishing farming and artistic
community near the confluence of the Chaudière and des
Fermes rivers, some 70 kilometres south of Québec City. It is
the principal town in a gently rolling area known as the
Beauce Country. Throughout this lovely, fertile realm, long
narrow swaths of farmland recall the old seigneurial system of
property division, and maple trees grow in colorful abundance.

Abenaki Indians were the original inhabitants. White
settlers arrived in 1736, when present-day St-Joseph was
established as a seigneury under Joseph Fleury de la
Gorgendière. De la Gorgendière named the land after the
Beauce region of his native France, and constructed a manor, a
small church, and a mill—the nucleus of a community that
has gradually become known as the "Cradle of the Beauce."
The seigneurial mill, near a waterfall on the Rivière des
Fermes, still stands, although in ruins.

The Chaudière's water plays a vital part in the life of St-
Joseph, nourishing the landscape and yielding rich clay
deposits that are used by La Céramique de Beauce—an artists'
cooperative—to create handsome pottery. But benevolent as
the river is, it also wreaks seasonal havoc. In spring and
autumn it overflows its banks, often flooding both the town
and the surrounding farmlands.

Nonetheless, St-Joseph is the Beauce Country's most
frequented tourist spot. A particular highlight for visitors is
the convent of the Sisters of Charity, which houses the Maison
des Artisans and the Marius Barbeau Museum. Barbeau, who
produced a number of books on French-Canadian and Indian
traditions and legends, was born at nearby Ste-Marie in 1883.
He died in 1969, in Ottawa, leaving behind a wealth of Québec
folklore knowledge. The museum honors this contribution.

The Cradle of the Beauce

MAPLE COUNTRY

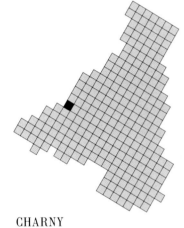

CHARNY

A light frosting of mist (*right*) clings to foliage overlooking the tumultuous waters of the Chaudière. *Chute* is French for waterfall—and this is the spectacular Chute de Charny.

Charny is a showcase of French colonial charm on the southern embankment of the St. Lawrence, 11 kilometres southwest of Lévis. The town traces its beginnings to the mid-17th century, and its steep-roofed houses with graceful dormer windows typify the architecture of that period. The town was named after Charles de Charny, the son of Jean de Lauzon, one-time governor of New France.

South of Charny, a diverse and colorful landscape of stony hills, gentle grasslands, prosperous farms, and prized fir and maple groves lines up against the horizon. This is the gateway to the Beauce Country—that long, magnificently fertile valley alongside the Chaudière River.

At times both gentle and fearsome, the Chaudière stirs the apprehensions of Charny residents with its seasonal moods. A helter-skelter of churning rapids and boiling whirlpools punctuates the last 100 kilometres of its snaking course, which—for the most part—Route 171 follows. Once in Charny, this ever-capricious river spreads suddenly, to almost half a kilometre in width, and flows over a rocky bed before plunging some 45 metres into a raging cauldron below—indeed, the name Chaudière derives loosely from the French word for cauldron: *chaudron*. This awesome view can be appreciated from the CN railway bridge or from the viaduct on Route 20. But the spectacle is most dramatic in Charny itself.

Here the Québec Ministry of Tourism has erected three lookouts onto the river and a roadside rest stop from which motorists can admire these breathtaking falls, all within six kilometres of the river's mouth. Before thrusting headlong into the St. Lawrence, the Chaudière makes one final serpentine flick of its tail, leaving in its wake a wide, curving estuary—and a quickened beat in the heart of anyone approaching this memorable sight for the first time.

Along a Raging River

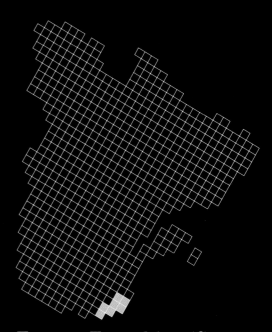

L'Estrie—or the Eastern Townships (Cantons de l'Est)—extends from the Richelieu to the Chaudière River, and from the St. Lawrence lowlands south to the Québec-Vermont border. Known as the "Garden of Québec," this vast and verdant realm nurtures many of the province's best dairy and livestock farms, as well as a number of highly productive apple orchards.

The Townships region was first settled in the 1790s by United Empire Loyalists fleeing north after the War of Independence. Then came waves of Irish, Scottish and English immigrants, followed by a large influx of French Canadians during the second half of the last century. Today l'Estrie is a predominantly French-speaking region.

L'Estrie's diverse landscape is a year-round mecca for outdoor enthusiasts. Freshwater lakes and fast-flowing rivers sustain water sports galore, from fishing to white-water rafting. The winter slopes of Mont Orford draw skiers by the thousands. During spring and autumn, the splendid scenery—gently rolling meadows, redolent maple and hardwood forests—charms a steady stream of nature lovers.

L'Estrie

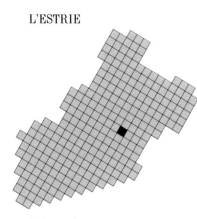

COOKSHIRE

Winter drapes the Cookshire area (*above* and *right*), a quiet domain of aging barns, weathered mills, and graceful homes dating back to the Loyalist era.

Quaint, pastoral, picturesque—such adjectives lend themselves easily to Cookshire's hillside setting, its century-old homes, its Gothic-style church, its gentle overview of the Eaton River. The town lies just 20 kilometres east of Sherbrooke, the nearest city, and was founded in the 1790s by settlers from New Hampshire and Vermont.

An antiquated covered bridge, erected by neighborhood farmers in 1838, spans the river just beyond the town. These "kissing bridges"—where many a man and his sweetheart sneaked embraces in the days of horse and buggy—are found throughout the Townships. (At the turn of the century, there were more than a thousand such bridges in Québec; today there are perhaps 80.) A number of fine old watermills also grace the rivers of this region. Many of these mills have stood for almost two centuries.

Within the town itself there are several historical buildings well worth seeing. These include the early 19th-century Bailey House, the Pope House (1863), the Old Post Office (1868), and a grocery store dating from 1851. A wool factory, on rue Principale, may also be visited. Appointments should be made in advance.

Cookshire is best known, however, for its annual bread festival. Each June the air around the town becomes permeated with the aroma of freshly baked bread. Loaves are prepared by the townswomen according to traditional family recipes and baked in large, outdoor ovens. Visitors from throughout the area flock to this event to sample different types of bread and share in the delicious country supper that is served at the end of the festivities.

An Aroma of Fresh-baked Bread

L'ESTRIE

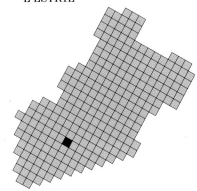

MONT ORFORD

Parc du Mont-Orford (*above*), a place of exceptional loveliness. From here several hiking trails wind to the top of Mont Orford and a scenic view of the surrounding countryside. Plant and animal life typical of the Eastern Townships is abundant throughout the park.

There are subtle benefits to rehearsing outdoors (*right*). Instruments played in the open air convey a purer, more direct sound—although quieter than the "reflected" sound most of us are accustomed to hearing on radio or on records. Sunshine, of course, is always a bonus.

At 738 metres, Mont Orford is one of the highest peaks in the Eastern Townships. It lies 120 kilometres southeast of Montréal, between Eastman and Magog, and dominates the western fringe of Mont Orford Provincial Park. Some 20 challenging ski slopes wind down its southern face, meeting in a small, sheltered valley. A chair lift from here transports skiers and sightseers to the summit.

A few minutes' drive from Mont Orford, and still in the park, is the Orford Arts Centre. Maintained by the Jeunesses Musicales du Canada, this splendidly modern building sprang from remarkably humble roots—a plain canvas tent occupied (in 1951) by a handful of musicians. Today the center is temporary home to some 300 students, and in the past 30 years artists from throughout the world have performed during its annual summer festival of classical music. In 1983 alone, the center presented some 60 concerts.

Newcomers wandering through the surrounding woods are often gently surprised by the harmonies filtering through the foliage—the lonesome echo of a flute, the quick chirp of a violin, the tinkle of a distant harp. These sylvan strains come from huts among the trees, where students practice in solitude.

Having created a sanctuary for young musicians, the center went on to establish studios for potters, sculptors, painters and lacemakers. Thus it is that the Orford Arts Centre continues to forge a warm and vital relationship between artist and public, an essential link in the process of renewing traditional art in the province of Québec.

Of Music and a Mountaintop

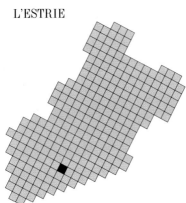

ST-BENOIT-DU-LAC

The Benedictine Abbey at St-Benoît-du-Lac (*above*): an echoing world of intricately tiled floors and graceful arches in mosaics of brick. St-Benoît was originally a monastery. It officially became an abbey in 1952.

Dusk presses against the old abbey (*right*), an other-worldly landmark in a realm of rich countryside. Fertile apple orchards, where summer visitors can pick their own fruits, surround the sanctuary.

The Benedictine Abbey at St-Benoît-du-Lac is a religious retreat overlooking Lac Memphrémagog. It was constructed as a monastery in 1912 and displays a handsome combination of octagonal and square towers, triangular gables, and narrow pointed windows. Its buildings are of pink granite.

The abbey's design was influenced by French-born Dom Paul Bellot, who immigrated to Canada in 1937 and became one of Québec's foremost ecclesiastical architects. He introduced a series of handsome modifications to the structure in the 1940s, when the monastery was being converted into an abbey. Bellot's grave is in the abbey grounds.

Home to some 60 monks of the Saint-Pierre-de-Solesme congregation, the abbey and its surrounding lands are a place of earthly and spiritual grace. The cloisters echo with the haunting harmonies of Gregorian chants, and on Sundays the public is invited to attend services. The monks produce all their own food, and in season sell fruit and vegetables. The abbey is also known for its cheeses: Ermite, St-Benoît and Ricotta.

This corner of the Eastern Townships is popular at all times of year. Magog, 16 kilometres north, is a charming community of cosy inns, quiet antique shops, and inviting bistros and restaurants. Brome Lake, one of the region's loveliest holiday resorts, is situated 20 kilometres to the west. Closer by, on the upper western shore of Lac Memphrémagog, is the tiny farming village of Austin. From an observation point at the foot of nearby Mont Chagnon, an awe-inspiring panorama of the area unfolds. To the north are the Orford Mountains, and in the south the famous Green Mountains of Vermont.

Far From the Madding Crowd

SOUTH BOLTON

Autumn displays its colors (*above*) along the banks of the Missisquoi Nord. Maple trees grow throughout the South Bolton area, and in summer and early fall roadside stands offer a variety of maple-sugar products.

A region famed for its rural charm (*right*), the Townships abounds in such pastoral images. Its scenic lakes, rivers and mountains make it a popular year-round holiday spot.

South Bolton, tucked away in a rural corner just west of Lac Memphrémagog, near the Québec-Vermont border, has fewer than 500 residents and, at first glance, little other to recommend it than a general store and a service station. Yet, in its smallness, South Bolton embodies a beguiling simplicity that is typical of the Eastern Townships.

Situated on the banks of the Missisquoi Nord, the village invites the attention of any passing sightseer with a camera and an eye for the picturesque. Old, dignified homes fronted by stately shade trees line the side streets. The main road is dominated by a large white church that is almost too big for its handful of parishioners. Green, gently rolling hillsides surround the settlement. It is somewhat surprising that such a lovely area is so sparsely populated, but much of the local countryside is densely wooded and the soil too poor for large-scale farming.

Most of the residents—as well as those in neighboring Henryville, Highwater, Sawyerville, Georgeville, and Sutton—are descendants of United Empire Loyalists who moved north after the War of Independence. They settled here at the beginning of the 19th century, clearing the land for crops, and building lumber mills, flour mills, and schools and churches. Their imprint has been a lasting one: the results of their endeavors can be glimpsed not only here, but throughout the Townships.

Mont Sutton and Bunker Hill, both popular ski areas, overlook this gentle community. Some 35 kilometres northeast is the town of Magog, a year-round sports center and the gateway to Parc du Mont-Orford.

Tiny, Simple, Unforgettable

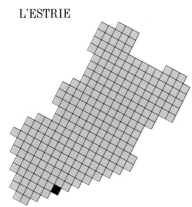

MANSONVILLE

Heart of the country (*above*): a grazing ground on the outskirts of Mansonville. During the warmer months, many of the farms in this region sell their produce at stalls set up along the roadside. Homemade preserves and luscious apples are among the traditional offerings.

An early morning haze rises from the Mansonville countryside (*right*). In winter this flat, sparsely treed terrain is excellent for cross-country skiing.

United Empire Loyalists founded Mansonville at the beginning of the 19th century, and with Vermont only a few kilometres to the south, it has retained much of the original flavor those fleeing Americans brought with them. Many of the village's 1,600 residents—like those of nearby Beebe, Stanstead, Rock Island, and Highwater—shop, vacation, visit friends and relatives, and even work, in the United States.

Mansonville's appearance typifies that of numerous other border settlements in the Eastern Townships: white-spired chapel, indispensable general store, and handsome colonial-style houses. The village is situated in the heart of a densely wooded mountain region, which was once a prime lumbering center. Sawmills along the border operated continuously to fill orders for domestic and U.S. customers. Excessive felling of trees and a decline in the lumber market, however, combined to make these enterprises all but obsolete. Today Mansonville has little industry apart from a handful of small privately owned farms.

Two popular ski resorts, just outside the village, bring a touch of vibrance to the area each winter. Mont Glen, almost midway between Mansonville and Knowlton, is a favorite center for novice and intermediate skiers. Nearby Owl's Head ranks with Mont Orford as one of the region's finest ski hills, attracting both beginners and experts. Its chair lift operates year-round, carrying visitors to the summit of Owl's Head and an exhilarating vista of Lac Memphrémagog and the Green Mountains of Vermont.

Down Along the Border

L'ESTRIE

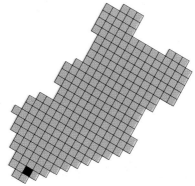

FRELIGHSBURG

The indestructible old flour
mill at Frelighsburg (*right*), a
handsome survivor from the
19th century. The mill has been
entirely restored.

Approaching Frelighsburg from the north, Route 213 crests
the brow of a low hill then descends steeply into the village
below. A stately 19th-century Anglican church with a shining
spire stands at the entrance to the community. Beside it, the
road enters a narrow two-lane bridge over the Pike River, and
then wends its way up the opposite face of the valley, passing a
number of clapboard homes, a small hotel, and a handful of
stores and restaurants. A few kilometres farther on, the road
crosses the Québec-Vermont border.

Many of the United Empire Loyalists who founded
Frelighsburg, in 1813, were Dutch emigrés from New York
State. Most of these settlers established themselves along the
river, building flour and wool mills. Forestry, however, was the
major local industry, and it gave the village a measure of
regional importance. But with time, those thick woods that
once fed the area's lumber mills fell to the axmen, leaving
today's residents a legacy of denuded grassland that extends
along both sides of the river to Vermont. Nowadays apples are
the area's principal cash crop.

The village's pioneer days live on in its splendidly
preserved flour mill, which stands on the riverbank beside a
shady phalanx of weeping willows. In neighboring Stanbridge,
Loyalist mementos are displayed in a museum operated by the
Missisquoi Historical Society. Visitors can wander through
replicas of a blacksmith's shop, a cobbler's shop, and a doctor's
office, all reflecting the lifestyle of the last century.

A Legacy of Grassland

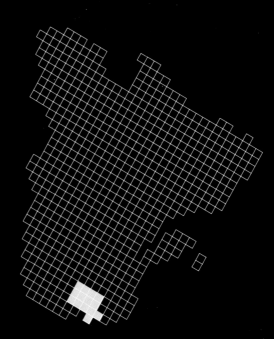

The Richelieu River rises in Lake Champlain, on the Québec-Vermont border, and flows almost due north for 130 kilometres before merging with the south shore of the St. Lawrence at Sorel. En route, it passes through a lovely, tranquil region where cosy pubs rub shoulders with ancient battle sites, and imposing stone fortresses invite visitors to picnic on their grounds.

Throughout this lush valley, pastoral settlements such as St-Ours, St-Charles, and St-Denis nestle among orchards and rich farmlands. Yet, serene as they are today, many of these villages bear the scars of a turbulent past, for it was here that much of the fighting in the Rebellion of 1837 took place. Monuments in a number of the area's communities commemorate the event.

Even before the rebellion, other skirmishes attended the landscape. In 1609 explorer Samuel de Champlain traveled upriver to battle the Iroquois. In 1760 an English force advanced downriver to Montréal and, fifteen years later, American soldiers followed the same route. During the War of 1812, Americans again invaded the region.

Visitors today can savor much of this history at two handsomely preserved forts, at Chambly and on Ile-aux-Noix. Both strongholds are situated on the banks of the Richelieu.

Richelieu/South Shore

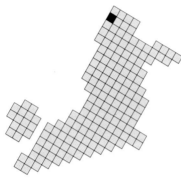

SOREL

The Sorel Islands (*above*), a network of waterways known well to fishermen and duck hunters.

Waterfront grain elevators at Sorel (*right*), a town humming with naval construction and related industries. Near here, a provincial marina berths more than 300 boats.

The Sorel Islands have long been a favorite haunt of duck hunters and bird watchers. Located at the entrance to Lac St-Pierre, these green patches of land range throughout a long marshy corridor which from spring to fall becomes a lively breeding ground for large colonies of waterfowl. As well as ducks, congregations of bustards, snipes, marsh wrens and common gallinules populate the area.

About 100 islands in all form a maze-like configuration of waterways, suddenly wide, then suddenly narrow. In some spots the waters are so heavily fringed with grasses that they are navigable only by flat-bottomed boats. In the deeper areas of the lake, pike and sturgeon abound, providing challenging sport for local fishermen. These fish are frequently served in the region's restaurants, in a popular seafood fricassee known as *gibelotte de poissons.*

Some of the islands, such as Ile Madame and Ile de Grâce, support tiny communities. Others are barely large enough to beach a boat on. Two of the islands—Ile aux Fantômes and Ile d'Embarrass—are accessible by road. A number of aging houses line the route to these insular settlements.

On the mainland opposite the islands, at the confluence of the St. Lawrence and Richelieu rivers, stands the town of Sorel itself, a busy inland seaport. This south shore settlement is an important shipping stop between Québec City, Montréal and Lake Champlain, in the United States.

A Maze of Green Islands

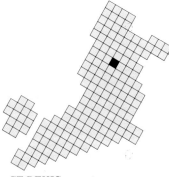

ST-DENIS

Armed defiance (*above*), a fitting monument to St-Denis' *Patriotes*. Men, women and children alike played a role in the fierce encounter here in 1837.

Right: The village of St-Denis, tranquil now along the banks of the Richelieu, a river that tells little of this pastoral community's turbulent past.

St-Denis, a historic farming village of 900 inhabitants, is situated on ancient seigneurial lands dating to 1694 and surrounded by a rich and verdant countryside noted for its peaceful splendor. Yet almost 150 years ago, this tranquil landscape was torn by strife. The first stop on the "Way of the Patriotes," St-Denis was a kindling point of the Lower Canada Rebellion of 1837.

Today's visitors will see elegant stone houses and tree-shaded streets, a magnificent double-spired church dating to 1796, a river rolling lazily by. During the rebellion, however, some 200 *Patriotes* fought an intense battle here against a force of 500 British soldiers. The engagement lasted six hours, and resulted in victory for the insurgents. The triumph, however, was short-lived—a year later the British returned and set fire to the village.

A cairn in the village marks the site of the Maison St-Germain, the big stone house in which the rebels barricaded themselves. In nearby Parc St-Denis, a larger than life statue of a *Patriote* in fighting stance commemorates 12 men killed in the battle.

Guided tours of the village's several historic buildings give present-day visitors a vivid sense of the community's past. From the waterfront, a ferry crosses the Richelieu to nearby St-Antoine, ancestral home of George Etienne Cartier, one of the Fathers of Confederation.

A Historic Kindling Point

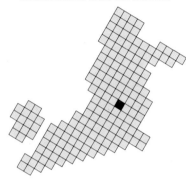

ROUGEMONT

Springtime warms the slopes of Mont Rougemont (*above*). In days to come the hillside will be emblazoned with the pink hues of ripening apple blossoms.

The fruits of summer (*right*), a timely prompter for Rougemont village's annual mid-August apple festival.

More than a hundred apple orchards array themselves on the gently rolling plain at Mont Rougemont's base. Around mid-May each year, they burst into bloom, flooding the plain with an ocean of delicate pink blossoms, and treating passing motorists to a vision of evanescent beauty.

The mountain is located some 40 kilometres east of Montréal, on the border of Rouville and St-Hyacinthe counties. It stands 400 metres high and shelters a long, lush valley which stretches almost all the way to St-Paul d'Abbotsford, 15 kilometres east.

This fertile area, sandwiched between the Marieville plain and the Yamaska River, once belonged to the 18th-century seigneury of Vaudreuil, which then encompassed the parishes of Rougemont, St-Paul d'Abbotsford, St-Pie, l'Ange-Gardien, St-Césaire and St-Damase. In the early 1800s Empire Loyalists from the United States settled the countryside en masse, no doubt impressed by a region so favorable to the cultivation of fruit and vegetables.

In mid-August, an apple festival animates the village of Rougemont. An interpretation center demonstrates apple-growing methods and exhibits products derived from the fruit. The following month a variety of produce stalls pop up along the roads, inviting tourists to stop and sample the wares. A few of these stands remain open all year round.

Not far from the village, more than 5,000 apple trees grow in the orchards at the Cistercian abbey of Notre-Dame de Nazareth, founded in 1932 by French monks from the Iles de Lérins, just off the coast of Cannes, in France. Visitors can wander through the abbey's chapel and shop at a small store where apples and cider are sold. Accommodation is available for travelers wishing to stay the night.

An Ocean of Apple Blossoms

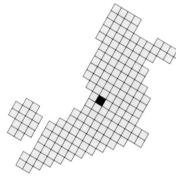

CHAMBLY

Churning water and fleecy clouds (*above*): the Richelieu's rapids at Chambly. This turbulent energy has been bypassed by the Chambly Canal, whose oldest locks date to 1843.

Right: The long robes of evening trail across the vivid Chambly sky. A place of history and constant beauty.

Chambly, with a population of 15,000, is one of the fastest growing communities on the south shore of the St. Lawrence. It is admirably situated on the banks of the Richelieu, and at the juncture of several major highways.

Chambly's advantageous location—where the river vaults over a series of shallow rapids before forming a deep basin— established it as a crossroads of history. Waves of explorers, warriors and invaders made their way up this water route, only to be detained by the rapids. The first explorer to penetrate this area of the Richelieu River Valley was Samuel de Champlain, in 1609.

It was not until 1665, however, when Capt. Jacques de Chambly erected Fort St-Louis (across from the rapids), that Europeans began to settle the area. This wooden fortification, built initially to repel Iroquois raids, was replaced in 1711 by a massive stone fortress. The fort today has been handsomely preserved. Three of its high curtain walls have been rebuilt, and a fourth partially reconstructed. Other structures on the grounds have been completely restored.

Although the rapids provided a strategic location for a fort, they were a hindrance to commercial travel. To facilitate navigation, the Chambly Canal was constructed in 1843. The canal remained essential to trade until the end of the last century. But with the arrival of the railway and the autoroutes, river commerce declined, and today the canal is principally a passageway for pleasure boats. Once coveted and fiercely fought over, Chambly now displays its rich beauty and heritage to appreciative tourists.

Passageway for Pleasure Boats

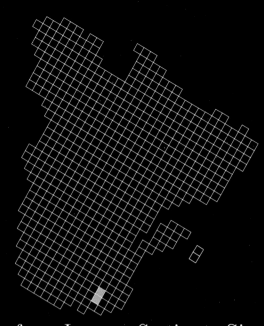

Early explorers, from Jacques Cartier to Sieur de Maisonneuve, were quick to recognize the value of Montréal's natural setting. With a stately mountain for a backdrop, and the St. Lawrence on its doorstep, it was an ideal location to found a community.

In the 1700s the settlement was a major fur-trading center. By 1832, the growing town had a population of 40,000. Today, with the recent merging of its 29 municipalities, Montréal is home to almost 2,800,000 citizens. It is the second largest city in Canada, and the largest French-speaking city in the world after Paris. Indeed, it is often referred to as "the Paris of North America."

An excellent network of highways, two large airports, a busy port, and a modern subway ("Le Métro")—these are but a few of the ingredients that ensure Montréal's continuing status as a world city. But more than that, Montréal is a city renowned for its Gallic charm—its *joie de vivre*. And it is this, above all else, that makes this spirited metropolis a perennial favorite with tourists from all over.

Montréal

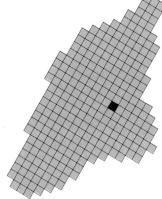

MOUNT-ROYAL

Mount-Royal Cemetery, from an unusual angle (*above*). A mere five-minute walk from here lies Beaver Lake, a lively playground area on the edge of Mount-Royal Park.

Dawn slowly lifts the darkness from the sleeping city of Montréal, exposing a view from the top of Mount Royal (*right*). Two million people live on the 50-kilometre-long island; another 800,000 inhabit the adjacent areas.

Thanks to a generous blessing of greenery, and the foresight of a unique man, Montréal today enjoys a verdant piece of country in its midst. Lounging gracefully on the grassy slopes of a long-extinct volcano, Mount-Royal Park was the inspiration of Frederick Law Olmstead, an American landscape architect and early conservationist. Olmstead conceived the park as a place free from the intrusion of man-made structures of any kind, and fought hard to implement this idea (as he also did with New York's Central Park).

The park was inaugurated in 1876, and in the years that followed, despite attempts to introduce unnecessary roads and buildings into the park, Olmstead's vision was largely respected. Only minor departures—such as an esplanade offering a panoramic view of the city, and two chalets where skaters and cross-country skiers can enjoy a snack and a hot drink—have impinged on the original plan.

In the last twenty years, a reforestation project has increased the number of trees on the mountain to 90,000. A few hectares of grassland, from the Mount-Royal Cemetery, have also been added. The sum total is an exquisite place of sanctuary—a world where Montrealers can stroll in solitude along leafy paths, relax beside a miniature lake, or simply picnic on the grass.

Popular with Montrealers of all ages, the park is especially favored by joggers. Throughout the summer months—and even in winter—these intrepid athletes make their way up the steep pathway that leads to the Mount-Royal Cross. This 30-metre illuminated landmark crowns Mount Royal, a fitting benediction for a place of such loveliness.

A Single Vision, Shared by All

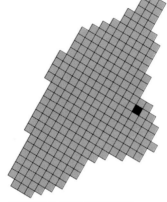

NOTRE-DAME CHURCH

Optical illusion—or reflection of history (*above*)? The immense facade of Notre-Dame mirrored in the windows of a modern office building in Place d'Armes.

A profusion of gold and sculpture (*right*) bedecks the interior of old Notre-Dame Church. Concerts are held here regularly, often featuring major figures of the music world.

Notre-Dame Church, in Place d'Armes, is one of Old Montréal's proudest and most preferred tourist destinations. Its history dates back some 300 years. But what visitors see today is actually a church in its third incarnation.

Around 1670 the wooden chapel of the Hôtel-Dieu—Montréal's first hospital—became too small to accommodate the swelling ranks of its parishioners. A larger church was built in 1683, but this too eventually proved inadequate, for by 1820 many of Montréal's 22,000 churchgoers were obliged to hear mass from the street outside the church. Plans were made for a basilica large enough to hold 7,000 worshipers, and Irish-American architect James O'Donnell was hired.

Drawing inspiration from the Notre-Dame Cathedral in Paris, O'Donnell saw the church through to completion in 1829. Twin spires, 70 metres high, were added 14 years later. The eastern tower—called Temperance—has a carillon of ten bells; the western tower—Perseverance—houses "le gros bourdon," a solitary bell weighing almost 12 tonnes.

Entering the church, one is immediately overwhelmed by the exquisite interior—by its pale blue, gold-flecked ceiling, its painted columns and profusion of ecclesiastical sculptures, and its vividly colored stained-glass windows and murals. It is a palace of excellences. Yet the whole breathtaking effect somehow manages to avoid ostentation.

The magnificently ornate high altar is the combined creation of many artists. Six statues of prophets surround the pulpit, and statues of angels flank the tabernacle. The 14 stained-glass windows, crafted in Limoges, France, depict religious themes and glimpses of early Montréal history. Behind the main altar is the Sacre-Coeur Chapel. Ravaged by fire in 1978, it has since been rebuilt in contemporary style.

A Palace of Excellences

CLOSSE

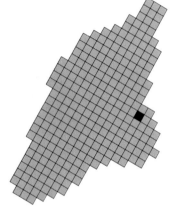

PLACE D'ARMES

Detail of the de Maisonneuve monument (*above*) shows Lambert Closse, Sieur de Maisonneuve's lieutenant, and the dog named Pilote. The monument, erected in 1895, marks the spot where an early Iroquois attack was successfully repulsed during the founding days of Montréal.

King, queen and the curious (*right*). At the foot of the de Maisonneuve monument, battlers today fight on a chessboard, a common summer pastime in Place d'Armes.

To a casual visitor, Place d'Armes may seem at first glance to be little more than a gracefully aging square on the edge of Old Montréal. Yet behind its gentle facade lies a history that spans almost 350 years: It was here, in 1644, that Sieur de Maisonneuve, founding governor of Montréal, defended his fledgling settlement against a fierce Iroquois attack; the morning of September 8, 1670, saw the last ragged vestiges of the French army, led by the Marquis de Vaudreuil, capitulating to the English; in later years, during the Rebellion of 1837, the square was a turbulent meeting place for *Patriote* insurgents.

It was not until the mid-19th century, however, that Place d'Armes reached its zenith—as the financial center of Montréal. Banks sprang up. Insurance firms established themselves. Lawyers and accountants took up offices. Hotels, restaurants, and crowded cafés made their way along side streets, and elegant homes flowered nearby. Dominating the area was the splendid edifice of Notre-Dame Church, a cherished monument that has endured to this day.

Lawyers still maintain offices in Place d'Armes (the square is only a minute's walk from the sparkling modernity of the municipal court building), and accountants, bankers, and insurance brokers still conduct business in the area. Yet nowadays much of the financial bustle has gone elsewhere. Horse-drawn calèches rattle across the square, and tourist buses pull up periodically, a small but fitting homage to the area's former glory.

Where Elegance Once Flowered

MONTREAL

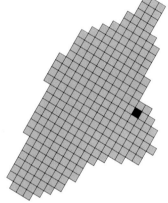

BONSECOURS MARKET

A copper statue of the Virgin Mary (*above*), adorns the rear of Notre-Dame-de-Bon-Secours Chapel and looks out over the harbor. Known as the sailors' chapel, the shrine has long been a landmark for mariners. The chapel stands adjacent to Bonsecours Market.

The famous dome of Bonsecours Market (*right*), witness to a long parade of history. The dome was damaged by fire in the 1970s and has since been restored.

From the 1880s till the mid-1960s, Bonsecours Market and its street and square seldom lacked the lively sounds, smells and colors of farmers, shoppers and fresh, ripe produce. Today, Bonsecours' cut stones and tall white colonnade are more likely to echo the clip-clop of a horse-drawn calèche or the bursts of laughter from the sidewalk cafés ringing nearby Place Jacques-Cartier. Strollers window-shop the boutiques and art galleries on cobbled St-Paul Street. An appetizing aroma occasionally escapes from one of the many fine restaurants in the neighborhood.

Completed in 1845, Bonsecours Market is a huge structure extending more than a block along the south side of St-Paul in Old Montréal. This Classic Revival building with its massive cupola and temple-like portico is nowadays closed to sightseers, but the view from outside and the historic setting make it well worth a visit.

The Palais de l'Intendance, the first building to be erected on this site, in 1648, was the residence of the governor and his administrative staff. By the early 1800s a Masonic Hall, a theater, and a hotel had replaced the Palais. In 1843 the hotel was gutted by fire; a year later the theater was torn down; and finally, in 1845, the land was cleared and the foundations of what was later to become Bonsecours Market were laid.

The parliaments of Upper and Lower Canada met in the partly completed building in 1849 and remained here until 1852 when Bonsecours Market became the city hall as well as police and fire headquarters. In 1878, the city hall moved to nearby Notre-Dame Street, and the market's interior was then converted into a spacious general marketplace, with the name Marché Bonsecours carved over the entranceway. It remained a market until 1964 when the building was completely refurbished and reopened as a municipal office building.

Cornerstone of History

MONTREAL

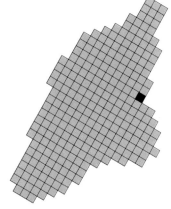

THE OLYMPIC PARK

The Olympic Stadium, packed almost to capacity (*above*). This splendid, modern-day arena can seat 60,517 spectators. Still missing are the tower and folding roof that will permit the stadium to be used for both indoor and outdoor events.

Competitors in the Montréal Marathon (*right*), emerging from the Jacques-Cartier Bridge. The Marathon was established a few years after the Montréal Olympics, and now attracts runners from all over the world.

Montréal played eager host to the XXIst Olympics during the summer of 1976, and although the Games are now a proud memory in Montréal's past, the Olympic Park remains a vital part of this cosmopolitan city. Since the opening, more than twenty million people have attended a vast spectrum of activities here, from Expo baseball games to large consumer-product fairs and religious gatherings.

The Olympics began in mid-July and ended just two weeks later. In that brief but frenetic period, throngs of fervent tourists and sports enthusiasts flocked to the newly constructed stadium, vélodrome, and swimming pools, and to other nearby facilities such as the Maisonneuve Sports Centre and the Maurice Richard Arena. The modernistic Olympic village provided comfortable accommodations for some 6,000 athletes, and satellite television brought the dramatic spectacle daily into the homes of more than one billion viewers in countries throughout the world.

Today, an informative staff is almost always on hand to guide newcomers around the site, explaining methods of construction, architectural innovations, and the specific function of each building. Visitors can enjoy a favorite sports activity, swim in the Olympic pool, and even dine on the site.

A subway station right in the heart of the park gives easy access to all the facilities. In summer, picnickers and sunbathers frequent the park; in winter cross-country skiers and snowshoers flock to its grounds.

In the Wake of the Olympics

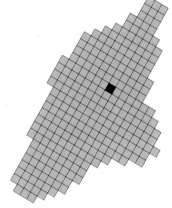

THE MARKETS

The best and freshest of the fruits of autumn (*above*), here displayed at a stall on St. Lawrence Boulevard. "The Main," as this famous street is called, is one of the busiest and ethnically richest spots in all of Montréal.

A bounty of ripe tomatoes (*right*), under the careful inspection of a customer at the Jean-Talon Market. This is the biggest of all Montréal marketplaces, and the most popular.

Outdoor markets, with their lively banter and colorful wares, have long been objects of fascination, and Montréal's marketplaces are no exception. Indeed, in recent years, both open-air and permanent indoor public markets have regained much of their former popularity here—catering, to a great extent, to the city's various ethnic communities. Pick almost any of these marketplaces, and you are likely to hear Italian, Greek, Portuguese, and Oriental languages mingling with French and English as shoppers peruse displays of mouth-watering foodstuffs from all over the globe.

Montréal's earliest marketplace sprang up around Place Royale, in the 1670s. Although that market is now a thing of the past, the square remains an integral part of Old Montréal. In the early 1800s, nearby Place Jacques-Cartier became the new focal point for marketgoers, even after the construction of adjacent Bonsecours Market. Noisy and energetic and bordered by taverns and restaurants, it was further enriched by strolling musicians, street hawkers and quack doctors. Nowadays, musicians and jugglers still carry on the tradition—often oblivious to its origins—in the old square.

Montréal has three major permanent markets today: Maisonneuve, Atwater, and Jean-Talon. Added to these are about 40 small market stalls which pop up regularly near certain Métro stations. Municipal authorities have heartily endorsed this recent resurgence of public markets and have even encouraged their development by granting more space to merchants and modernizing existing locations.

A Colorful Tradition Revived

MONTREAL

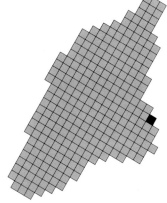

LA RONDE

Fireworks (*above*) are a nightly feature at Man and His World. But on special occasions—St-Jean-Baptiste Day (June 24) and Canada Day (July 1)—the displays are even more glorious than usual.

What child can fail to be enthralled by the bright lights and fast rides of La Ronde (*right*)? But the pleasure park is a favorite spot with adults too. Daily, weekly, or seasonal passes are available.

Ile Ste-Hélène is a lively recreational retreat in the middle of the St. Lawrence. It was originally named by Samuel de Champlain in honor of his wife, Hélène, and in 1657 became part of the Seigneury of Longueuil, one of the most prestigious estates in New France. This arrangement lasted until 1818, when the British crown, threatened by the prospect of a U.S. invasion, purchased the island for $65,000. The British fortified Ile Ste-Hélène, making it Montréal's first line of defense against naval attack. Access was then restricted until the Canadian government took possession in 1876.

During the 1960s the surface area of Ile Ste-Hélène was more than doubled for Expo 67, when Ile Ronde to the east and Ile Verte to the west were linked to it by vast landfill causeways. The world's fair lasted only one season, but the site continued to delight visitors for many years after, under the name of Man and His World. Several countries, among them France, India, Iran, and China, kept up pavilions. But eventually all of these structures were converted to other uses, or simply demolished. However, one remarkable Expo landmark holds the attention of sightseers to this day. The Geodesic Dome, once the much-admired U.S. pavilion, is almost as striking as it was in 1967—despite a fire that ravaged its outer protective covering in 1976.

Although the heady atmosphere that reigned during the Sixties is gone forever, the island still remains a popular Montréal drawing card. The old British fort now houses the Montréal Military and Maritime Museum, as well as La Poudrière, a well-known Montréal dinner-theater. And in summer La Ronde becomes as crowded as ever. The aquarium, Fort Edmonton, and the Québecois Village endure as oft-visited playgrounds—as do the midway rides, favorites with "children" of all ages.

All the Fun of the Fair

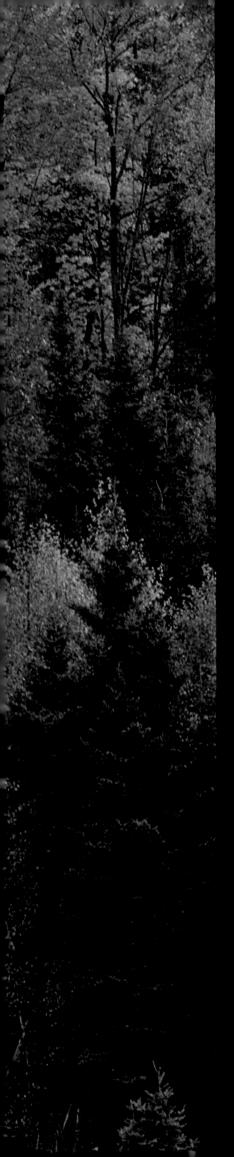

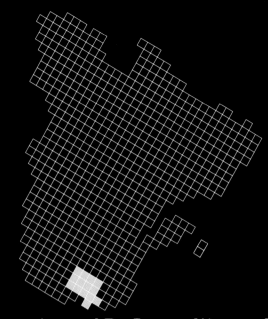

The adjoining regions of De Lanaudière and the Laurentians are two of Québec's most popular vacationlands, each with its own exceptional endowments. De Lanaudière delights visitors in search of the great outdoors, while the Laurentians seduce vacationers by providing holiday resorts *par excellence*.

At De Lanaudière's western limits, the historic Chemin du Roy follows the scenic course of the broad St. Lawrence River. Inland, the Joliette and Mastigouche wildlife reserves and vast Lac Taureau are the prime attractions. Thick, colorful maple groves abound throughout. The tobacco-growing plains between Mascouche and St-Barthélémi exude a quieter splendor.

Prophecies of eventual prosperity echoed throughout the Laurentians in the last century, and have long since rung true. For today this is one of the most highly developed vacation areas in North America, due in large part to superb skiing facilities. Long-established resorts are open year round in such communities as Val-Morin, Val-David, Ste-Agathe-des-Monts, and St-Jovite.

De Lanaudière and the Laurentians

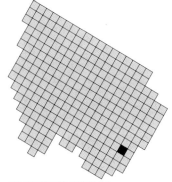

ST-JOSEPH-DU-LAC

The wrong time of year for a dip (*above*)—but in summer the entire St-Joseph-du-Lac area abounds with swimmers and boaters. Parc Paul-Sauvé, a short distance from the village, is a small and popular provincial park that invites just such activities.

A shy beginning (*right*): Springtime kindles a pale fire in the early foliage of an apple orchard. Apple trees provide some of the most striking seasonal colors in the St-Joseph-du-Lac area, as leaves change from delicate whites to sturdier shades of pink and red.

From its hillside setting, the peaceful farming village of St-Joseph-du-Lac looks out onto a splendid panorama of Québec countryside. The view stretches as far as Montréal, 40 kilometres east. Vaudreuil is also visible, as is the far shore of Lac des Deux Montagnes. The Oka hills and park dominate the foreground, and the surrounding landscape is an inviting mix of plains, hills, and tree-fringed streams.

Situated in one of the most fertile areas of Québec, the village dates to 1885. It was founded by settlers from the Montréal and Gatineau regions. Today its population of 2,200 prospers from local stud farms and a high yield of fruit and vegetable produce. Indeed, St-Joseph-du-Lac is known as the "Apple Kingdom," because of the multitude of orchards that flourish on the surrounding hillsides.

Springtime brings a blaze of blossoms to these hills. At harvesttime, toward the end of August, the annual apple festival is held. For a small fee, members of the public are invited into the orchards to pick apples. The point is not really to save a few dollars, but to commune with the sights and scents of nature on a fine summer day.

Swimming, sailing, and canoeing are popular summer pastimes along the sandy beaches of nearby Parc d'Oka. Cross-country skiing and snowshoeing are favorite winter activities. At the town of Oka, a Trappist monastery receives visitors who reserve in advance. On a nearby mountainside stand seven stone chapels that were built in 1740–42 as a Way of the Cross. This is the oldest calvary in Canada. Each year a small religious procession winds to the three main chapels grouped around the mountaintop.

An 'Apple Kingdom' in the Hills

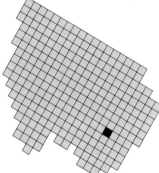

MONT-ROLLAND

Mont-Rolland in winter (*above*), a scene strikingly at odds with that shown in the photograph opposite. Autumn has its delights, but snow brings its own rewards: Cross-country ski trails abound throughout the area, and more than 100 ski lifts and tows await slope-hungry downhillers.

Fall foliage and mirror lake (*right*). In early October, during the *Fête des Couleurs* (Festival of Colors), visitors flock to this area to celebrate just such scenery. This splendid picture-show rarely lasts more than a week; after that the leaves have dropped for another winter.

Sheltered within a natural amphitheater and surrounded by hills near the Rivière du Nord, the Laurentian village of Mont-Rolland is renowned as a skier's paradise. Some 20 major downhill ski areas lie within easy reach. Cross-country skiing is equally popular, with such well-known trails as Maple Leaf, Johannsen, Gillespie, Wizard, and Fleur de Lys located nearby. Some of these cross-country trails extend as far as the Ottawa River Valley.

Each winter the Mont-Rolland downhill ski festival draws lively crowds of ski enthusiasts together for a memorable weekend of competitions and social events. But skiing is by no means all these pleasure-packed Laurentian mountains have to offer. Sightseeing is popular at all times of the year. And during the warmer months, the King, Plante, and Condor peaks provide challenging terrain for climbers, hikers, and campers alike.

The Condor Needle, 25 metres high and almost vertical, stands beside Mont Condor and is eastern Canada's only "needle" formation. The gap between the two landmarks can be climbed for about eight metres, to a point where it widens. Both rocks were formed of lava.

Mont-Rolland was one of the first of the lower Laurentian communities to be settled, in the 1840s. It was originally part of the parish of Ste-Adèle and—as was typical of these early Laurentian settlements—it relied on forestry and farming for income. In 1902, a paper industry was founded here, and 16 years later the municipality of Mont-Rolland was officially established. Although the village has grown considerably, its population is still only 2,300.

In Fall, a Pageantry of Foliage

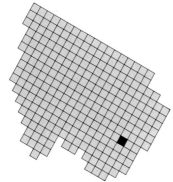

ST-JEROME

A small farm dwelling on the outskirts of St-Jérôme (*above*). In the last century the city's founding father, Curé Labelle, urged such homesteaders to stay on—that riches would eventually come from the land. Fortune has indeed smiled on Labelle's faith, although prosperity has come more from tourism than from crops.

The Rivière du Nord in winter (*right*), just outside St-Jérôme. Midwife at the birth of the settlement, the river now provides precious electricity to a thriving generation of descendants.

St-Jérôme, less than an hour's drive north of Montréal, is the entranceway to some of the finest year-round resort country in Québec. Established 150 years ago, the settlement began as a small wool- and flour-producing community on the banks of the Rivière du Nord. Today the same river provides hydroelectric power to St-Jérôme, which has blossomed into a spirited city of almost 30,000.

In the mid-1800s, shortly after St-Jérôme's founding, economic conditions became so dire here that many disheartened inhabitants left to work in New England. Yet despite these hard times, a farsighted local priest recognized the beauty of the Laurentian wilderness and determined to open the area to large-scale settlement. With unshakeable enthusiasm, Curé Antoine Labelle encouraged forlorn residents to stay, and enticed European immigrants to make their home here. During the 1870s and 1880s he created some 20 new parishes and persuaded a reluctant government to route the Montréal-Québec City railway through St-Jérôme.

When Curé Labelle died in 1891 he had seen farms take shape, villages grow, and St-Jérôme become a distribution center for surrounding new settlements. He had also witnessed, true to his initial vision, an inkling of the tourism that was to come. A bronze statue in the city's Labelle Park honors this Most Reverend "King of the North."

An even greater monument—the Cathédrale de St-Jérôme—also pays homage to Curé Labelle. The largest place of worship in the Laurentians, the cathedral went up between 1897 and 1899, and opened its doors a year later. Among its many splendid exhibits are a huge portable altar, a silver chalice presented by Pope Leo XIII, and a number of mementos relating to the beloved Curé of the Laurentians.

An Old Prophecy Fulfilled

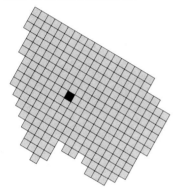

MONT-TREMBLANT

Red roof and snow and shining spire (*above*): simple, evocative, and colorful—yet not at all out of keeping with the picturesqueness that greets visitors in the Laurentians. One of the quaintest villages in the region is Mont-Tremblant itself, near the southern approach to the park.

A mere fraction of vast Mont-Tremblant park (*right*), caught by the camera. Beyond lies an even more remote area—the park's northern wilderness forest. Unmarked by roads or trails, it is a magnet for only the truest of fishermen and the boldest of canoeists.

Parc Mont-Tremblant is the oldest and most frequented of Québec's 35 parks and wildlife reserves. Its 250,000 hectares of rugged mountains, thick forests, and isolated lakes and rivers draws visitors from all over the province, as well as from other parts of Canada and the rest of the world.

The park is situated 140 kilometres north of Montréal and can be reached from several locations: St-Faustin, Labelle, St-Donat, or St-Côme. Within Mont-Tremblant, a well-developed nature interpretation center offers guided tours, film presentations, and lectures throughout the year. The center focuses on three zones—Rivière du Diable, Pimbina, and Assomption.

A sparkling constellation of some 380 lakes, cascading waterfalls, rushing rivers, and quiet streams invites bathing, sailing, canoeing, and fishing. Most fishermen bring their own boats, but the Québec Ministry of Recreation, Fish and Game rents them in certain locations. A number of the campgrounds have excellent sites, sized for individuals or small groups. In winter, the park beckons with invigorating cross-country and snowshoe trails and wide expanses of wilderness suitable for snowmobiling.

The village of Mont-Tremblant lies just outside the park, on the shores of Lac Mercier and near the base of the 960-metre mountain that gave both the park and the community its name. The Mont-Tremblant resort area, three kilometres northeast, boasts the highest downhill ski slopes in Québec. A number of cosy inns and fine restaurants are located throughout the area, as are several art galleries and handicraft boutiques.

Québec's Most Popular Park

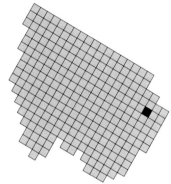

JOLIETTE

Tobacco leaves, freshly cut (*above*). Cigar, pipe, and flue-cured tobacco are the main types grown.

The Joliette countryside (*right*), a rich tobacco-producing region with an annual average of 125 frost-free growing days. Colorful hothouses and curing sheds decorate the landscape.

Joliette lies 75 kilometres northeast of Montréal, in the shadow of the ancient Laurentians. Rambling market gardens and quiet dairy farms cluster around its outskirts, and the Rivière L'Assomption flows by. Yet despite these pleasant, bucolic surroundings, the city is a bustling one, with a population of 23,000 and a flourishing textile and tobacco-manufacturing industry. The crop has been cultivated on a large scale in this region since the 1930s.

Renowned regionally as an educational and cultural center, Joliette attracts choirs of amateur singers and classical musicians to the annual Lanaudière Music Festival. The festival is held in summer, and many of the artists are 15 or younger. For drama enthusiasts, the Théâtre des Prairies stages a series of plays throughout the same season. Blessed with a touch of character, the theater is ensconced in a converted tobacco-drying shed.

Joliette is also endowed with a distinguished and much-visited art museum. Founded 25 years ago, the Joliette Museum of Art exhibits European and Canadian paintings, as well as sculpture and gold-crafted *objets d'art*. Its library holds more than a thousand rare books.

A long way from its roots, Joliette originated as a lumber town under the name of L'Industrie. A sawmill built at the edge of the river in 1823 fostered further growth, and in 1850 construction of a railway line from Lanoraie spurred development of several other parishes. Thirty years later the town was officially renamed.

A Rich Tobacco Heartland

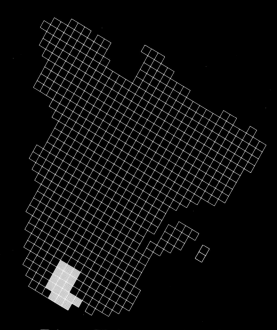

Québec's Ottawa River Valley region is a magnificent
expanse of lakes, rolling hills and forested terrain
north of the Ottawa River, across from the nation's
capital. Much of this land is shared by Gatineau Park
and by three large cities: Gatineau, Hull, and Aylmer.
Together these cities form a bustling metropolitan
community accounting for more than two-thirds of the
300,000 people within the region.

Settlement here has been relatively recent, a
number of towns having sprung up only after the turn
of the century. (A few communities—such as Aylmer—
however, date to the early 1800s.) In its earliest days
the region was much traveled by explorers—by men
such as Cartier, Champlain, and La Verendrye, who
relied on the Ottawa River to penetrate the land's
interior. Their route was soon followed by fur traders,
missionaries, and loggers. Today, of course, the
landscape is a world away from the forbidding
wilderness that confronted those long-ago voyagers.
Treacherous rapids have given way to modern bridges,
backbreaking portages to modern highways, and
untamed hillsides to modern ski slopes.

The Ottawa River Valley

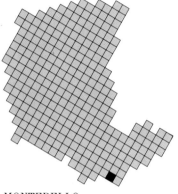

MONTEBELLO

Old and genteel, the historic Papineau House (*above*) gazes out onto the tranquil grounds of Montebello. The manor contains a wealth of antique memorabilia and is now used as a clubhouse.

A fresh fall of snow blankets the landscape of the Plaisance Wildlife Reserve (*right*). The park is a haven for winter sports enthusiasts and a paradise for nature lovers in summer.

The southeastern portion of the Ottawa River Valley region stretches for 30 kilometres along the north shore of the Ottawa River, and was once a thriving seigneury known as *La Petite Nation*. The seigneury was first settled around the end of the 18th century. Today some two dozen towns and villages speckle this lush valley, Montebello being the best known.

This charming resort and farming town takes its name from the imposing baronial mansion of Louis-Joseph Papineau, leader of the 1837 rebellion in Lower Canada. The stone manor, built here in 1850, and preserved as a museum, stands on the grounds of the Chateau Montebello Hotel. A chapel nearby holds the grave of Papineau. Another building—the "Grainerie"—was once the studio of Napoléon Bourassa, a 19th-century painter and sculptor whose works grace Notre-Dame-de-Bonsecours Church in Montréal.

The hotel itself is well worth a visit. Situated at the very heart of the old seigneury and surrounded by forests, lakes, and waterfalls, it epitomizes the elegant hunting-lodge style of 1930s architecture. It contains some 200 handsomely appointed rooms, and was host to the 1981 Western Economic Summit Conference. Guests entering the hotel are greeted by a towering octagonal hearth, which dominates the lobby.

Just outside Montebello lies the Plaisance Wildlife Reserve. This lovely but little-known sanctuary is an ideal spot for picnickers in summer, and an exhilarating wilderness for cross-country skiers and snowshoers in winter. At any time of the year, however, it is a nature lover's delight.

A Rebel-Leader's 'Little Nation'

THE OTTAWA RIVER VALLEY

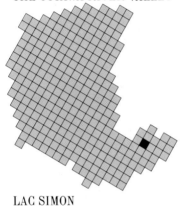

LAC SIMON

Rustic barn and snow-mantled roof, an image typical of the hushed, winter countryside surrounding Lac Simon (*above*). Near the north shore of the lake lies a region of equally enticing scenery, Papineau-Labelle Provincial Park.

Snowmobile tracks weave across the frozen surface of Lac Simon (*right*). At any time of year, the waters of this deep lake are unusually cold.

Set like a sparkling jewel in the heart of a pristine wilderness, Lac Simon extends from Chénéville to Duhamel, a distance of some 15 kilometres. Dense, forested highlands rise abruptly from its edge. In the middle of the lake lies Ile du Canard Blanc, and, at the center of this rocky island, yet another lake.

Visitors can travel for hours in any direction in the vast, game-filled wilderness surrounding Lac Simon and not meet a soul. Chénéville, one of the region's few towns, started out around 1867 as a mission post. Like most Ottawa River Valley communities of that time, the settlement carved its livelihood out of the thick, lumber-rich forest. Today Chénéville is a favorite spot for outdoor enthusiasts in search of exhilarating canoeing and fishing expeditions (trout and pike are particularly abundant). Outdoor theater and pleasure-craft sailing are also part of the Lac Simon bill of fare. In July, the annual Lac Simon "swim across" takes place. And, as is usual in a flourishing vacation resort, a local arts and crafts industry is also evolving.

Duhamel, on the lake's north shore, is an old woodland settlement of no more than 300 inhabitants. Income here is largely from the tourist trade—indeed, the village is known as the gateway to the Lac Simon Tourist Centre, a recreational park that serves a wide range of outdoor activities.

Ripon and St-André-Avellin—located to the west and north of Lac Simon—are two other much-frequented vacation communities with a similar feast of outdoor pleasures to offer. The area surrounding these two settlements is especially popular with winter sports buffs. Shortly after the first heavy snow, the landscape becomes quickly streaked with the tracks of cross-country skiers and snowmobilers.

A Lovely Lakeside Playground

THE OTTAWA RIVER VALLEY

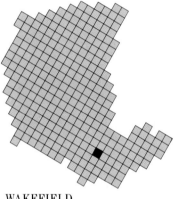

WAKEFIELD

An old covered bridge—the Gendron (*above*)—spans the Gatineau River and leads on into Wakefield and a world of splendid autumn foliage. The bridge is 88 metres long.

Time seems to stand still, here at the old MacLaren gristmill (*right*), while the waters of the Lapêche River rush on by. The mill is also known locally as the Fairbairn mill, after the original builder.

A 30-kilometre drive north of the Ottawa-Hull district leads back more than a century to a tiny Québec village with the decidedly English name of Wakefield. Situated on the banks of the Gatineau, this rustic community embraces a population of perhaps a hundred or so inhabitants. Most of these residents are directly descended from British immigrants who settled here in the early 1800s.

A century ago, an Austrian innkeeper who was both a skilled mason and cabinet maker constructed the local inn on a quiet road next to a small duckpond. Even after 100 years, details of the innkeeper's fine craftsmanship are evident. In winter the inn is frequented by skiers from the local slopes.

The true gem of Wakefield, however, is the fieldstone gristmill on the outskirts of town, next to the Lapêche River. Built by a Scotsman named William Fairbairn, the mill is three stories high and has remained solid on its stone foundations since 1838.

Six years after it was completed, the Fairbairn Mill was purchased by David MacLaren, who also established lumbering and brick-making businesses and a general store there. Today the mill and MacLaren's brick house—which stands on a bank above the mill—are maintained by the National Capital Commission. The buildings have been restored to their original state and are open to the public.

Not far from the mill, on a hill overlooking the village and the Gatineau River, is the MacLaren Cemetery. Canada's 19th prime minister, Lester Bowles Pearson, is buried within.

Reflections in an Old Millpond

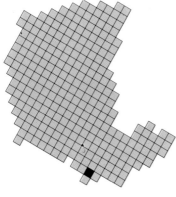

GATINEAU PARK

Lovely Gatineau Park (*above*) provides a delightful home for creatures great and small. The park was established in 1938, on land shaped by ancient glaciers. Some 12,000 years ago, all was ice.

Morning sunlight mingles with mist and trees (*right*) in Gatineau. Fires have left their mark on the forests of this vast park; most of Gatineau's trees are less than 65 years old.

Gatineau Park, a 35,000-hectare playground in the midst of an inviting wilderness, is a sanctuary for native plants and animals as well as a year-round recreation retreat for many thousands of visitors. The park lies within sight of Ottawa's Parliament Buildings, and straddles the confluence of the Gatineau and Ottawa rivers.

Spring here is heralded by the familiar sight of Canada geese winging across the skies. The woods come alive with croaking frogs, and muskrats and otters take to the marshes and ponds that dot this region. A hiker may come across fresh bear tracks in the mud of a beaver dam, or glimpse a deer, a fox, or a porcupine on the banks of a stream. The park's lakes and rivers teem with dore, pike, trout, and carp.

Other seasons produce their own unique and ever-changing spectrum of delights. Campers throng the area throughout summer. In October, when the hills are splashed with the flaming colors of autumn, thousands of city dwellers converge on the park. And from December to March, winter sports enthusiasts flock to the area.

Gatineau Park is divided into five sections: Lac des Fées, the Promenade, Lac Philippe, Lac La Pêche, and the Eardley area. The countryside around Lac des Fées, on the outskirts of Hull, offers spectacular scenery, as well as hiking, boating, and skiing. The Promenade region is the best known and the most frequently visited. Lac Philippe, some 30 kilometres from Hull, has superb beaches and fine camping sites, and attracts swimmers and snowshoers. The waters of Lac La Pêche are popular with fishermen. The last section, the Eardley area, consists of wooded hills and lakes, and a wealth of dramatic escarpments and plateaus.

A Spectrum of Outdoor Delights

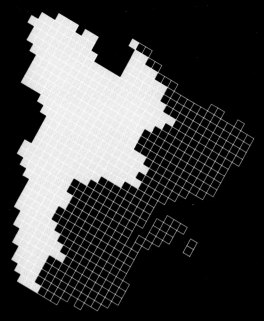

Northern Québec is a remote, snowbound hinterland of dense forests and tempestuous waterways. The terrain is endowed with a wealth of mineral resources, and the rivers offer unique potential for energy.

The Abitibi region extends 180 kilometres from the Ontario border to Senneterre. Most of the land is heavily forested. Over the past 30 years several small settlements here have prospered with the development of mining and lumber industries. The town of Amos lies in the heart of this mineral-rich region. After a railway opened up the area in 1914, the town became a gold mining center.

Témiscamingue is the southernmost region, its landscape the least harsh. Forests are a blend of both coniferous and deciduous trees. The area west of Rouyn is primarily farmland. From high on the banks of Lac Témiscamingue a vast, magnificent checkerboard of fields greets the eye.

Nouveau-Québec, by far the largest region in the province, is also the most uninviting—more than half of it is a silent, barren tundra rooted in permafrost. Yet Nouveau-Québec holds an irresistible fascination, and an undeniable challenge. It is only within the last two decades that humans have been able to make inroads on this land and harness its immense resources.

Abitibi-Témiscamingue, Nouveau-Québec/James Bay

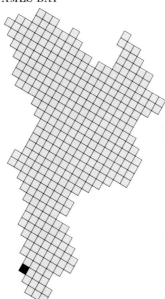

VILLE-MARIE

Ville-Marie (*above*), a gentle respite along a quiet highway. But there are always seasonal surprises. In summer, for example, travelers passing through can enjoy a colorful exhibition of local paintings, pottery, and copper enamel work.

The "enchanted forest" (*right*), a labyrinth of weirdly contorted trees sculpted by whimsical winds and an ungiving climate.

Ville-Marie is a remote northerly settlement of some 2,400 inhabitants, located near the Ontario border. Over the years the town has evolved into a regional tourist center, providing a warm welcome to travelers on the lonely road between Abitibi and the community of Témiscaming.

Two sites popular with visitors are the ruins of Fort Témiscamingue, which dates to 1720, and the Parks Canada interpretation center. But by far the most unusual spectacle in this area is the "enchanted forest." Here gnarled and grotesque tree trunks, created by the vagaries of nature, loom over the raw and sinewy landscape like twisted sentinels.

In August, the town hosts a three-day canoe race from the waterfront to North Bay, Ontario, 200 kilometres away. This is also the month when Ville-Marie holds a four-day commercial and industrial exposition. Locally made handicrafts are displayed, and Indians from the area exhibit beaded moccasins, necklaces, lamps and toys.

A little-known region, Abitibi-Témiscamingue is nonetheless a land of vast dimensions, characterized by enormous distances separating communities from each other. Settlement began in the mid-1800s, when lumberjacks learned of the region's virgin forests. The arrival of a railway in 1896 spurred further growth.

By 1929, the region's population was 34,000. But even here the effects of the Great Depression were harshly felt. The economy did not improve until the 1940s when the mining industry and pulp-and-paper mills were established.

Beside an Enchanted Forest

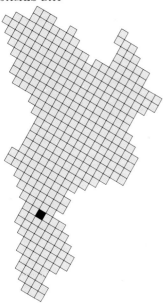

MATAGAMI

Trees in the Matagami region consist mainly of black spruce, gray pine, and short tamaracks (*above*). Because trees grow very slowly in this harsh northerly climate, lumbering is not practiced.

Matagami under snow (*right*). Winter temperatures in this area can drop as low as -50° Celsius. The average annual temperature is -4° Celsius.

Straight roads, prefabricated houses, trailer parks—Matagami is one of those distinctive Québec communities built entirely around the mining industry. It was developed next to Lac Matagami, according to precise blueprints, and is similar in appearance to Chibougamau, another frontier mining town some 220 kilometres east.

Matagami was incorporated in 1963. Before then, this vast plateau was a dense expanse of forestland. When exploration revealed concentrations of zinc, copper, and molybdenum beneath the ground, the town was born.

This area, on the eastern fringes of Abitibi, is part of the Laurentian shield. Altitude rarely exceeds 350 metres, and land and climate are demanding. Economic foundations often appear fragile, because of the precarious nature of the mining, as well as that of forestry and agriculture, but unshakeable drive and persistency keep the inhabitants of this corner of Québec optimistic. Nonetheless, for the past several years tourism has increased, and Matagami is now one of the stops on organized tours around Abitibi and the huge hydroelectric works of Nouveau-Québec.

As in most mining communities, Matagami's 4,500 residents have much in common. The majority know the history of the mines; their lives center around them. Mining is talked about on the radio, in the stores, whenever friends get together. Important news is a sudden fluctuation in the metal market. But beyond this shared interest lies something more profound. Living, as they do, some 800 kilometres north of Montréal, these modern-day pioneers thrive on direct and constant human communication. Special bonds of friendship bind many of the miners together. While not always understandable to visitors, these ties frequently last a lifetime.

A Town Built from Blueprints

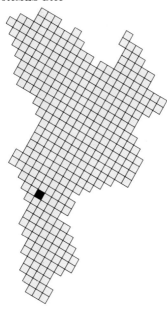

OPINACA

Two views of the Opinaca. The photograph above shows the river as it flows northeast of Fort Rupert, a tamed and silent-running waterway. On the right, a view more characteristic of this mighty river. Water accounts for almost 15 percent of the surface area of this northerly region.

Staggering in its remoteness, the Opinaca landscape spans more than 1000 square kilometres of wilderness and is heavily veined with rivers, lakes, and man-made reservoirs. A straight and solitary highway links this lonely region to Matagami and the outside world.

In 1971, Opinaca was the site of an unprecedented engineering task—to harness the virtually inexhaustible hydroelectric potential that lay dormant in the region. It was a project of epic dimensions. Hundreds of kilometres of roadways were built. Airports were hacked out of the bush. Bridges were erected, and modern communications facilities were installed. Whole towns sprang up overnight to accommodate the burgeoning population. At the peak of construction, at least 18,000 workers and their families swelled the area's six towns and five villages.

In the course of the project, the waters of the Eastmain and Opinaca rivers were redirected toward the La Grande Rivière. Funneled through the LG 2 complex, the combined force of these three vigorous young rivers can produce enough electricity to power an entire province. The system has been in full operation since 1980, when the various dams and hydroelectric installations were completed.

Although much of the landscape in the Opinaca region has been drastically altered by the project, the environment has not been overlooked. Both money and time have been set aside by the James Bay corporation to protect and restore this vast and fruitful wilderness.

A Magnificent Québec Epic

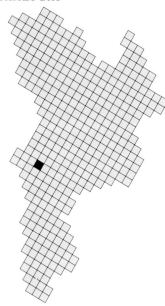

LG 3

Construction activity at its peak (*above*). Throughout this region, some 1500 kilometres of permanent roads and five major airports were built.

In this land of midnight sun, outdoor work continues all through the night in summer (*right*).

LG 3 is one of three mammoth generating stations on the La Grande Rivière. It forms part of the gigantic James Bay hydroelectric project. The La Grande itself is the largest body of water in the James Bay region. Its 800-kilometre length flows westward through 100,000 square kilometres of trackless wilderness—an area more than twice the size of Switzerland—before emptying into James Bay. The harnessing of this waterway, together with the partial annexation of three neighboring river basins (the Caniapiscau to the east, the Grande Baleine to the north, and the Opinaca to the south), has been a task that almost defies imagination.

The LG 3 powerhouse was built above ground on an island some 200 kilometres upstream from the mouth of the La Grande. Its dam system raises the water level immediately upstream from the station and this water is confined within a reservoir by 67 dikes. The reservoir alone has an area of 2460 square kilometres—more than two and a half times the area of Lac St-Jean.

To begin work on this monumental project it was first necessary to reroute, for a time, the flow of the La Grande. A two-phase plan was devised. The first phase, which took about 18 months, cut off the south arm of the river by means of two temporary man-made barriers. Thus excavation of the generating station was able to begin, along with construction of the south dam. The second phase closed off the north arm of the river and set a series of locks in place. This took three and a half years. Construction of LG 3 began in 1976. It was not until April 1981 that engineers and construction workers—and all others concerned—were able to wipe the dirt from their hands, proud of a job well done.

Powerhouse of the North

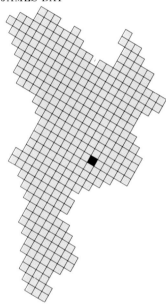

CANIAPISCAU

Out of a solid mass of stone (*above*), a new channel has been carved to augment the Caniapiscau's flow. Many of the rocks in this region date from the Precambrian Era, almost 2,500 million years ago.

After the disruptions of the Caniapiscau project, nature has been restored to its original state (*right*). Here, some 650,000 new trees and shrubs were planted throughout a 500-hectare area.

The Caniapiscau River rises high in the northern reaches of Québec, child of an icy no-man's-land west of Schefferville. Along its thundering northward journey toward Ungava Bay, it recruits the forces of several other powerful rivers, as well as the waters of two large lakes. The resulting torrent is awesome.

As befits a mighty river, Caniapiscau is the name that was also given to one of the biggest construction sites in the James Bay hydroelectric project. Encompassing a territory of more than 10,000 square kilometres, the gigantic undertaking required a full-time team of more than 4,000 workers, and cost over a billion dollars.

The task began with the diverting of the upper watershed of the Caniapiscau toward the La Grande Rivière, in the southwest. Then an enormous 4350-square-kilometre reservoir—almost twice the size of that at LG 3 (*page* 140)—was created to corral this new source of power.

Two massive dams were erected to guard the reservoir and protect the neighboring valleys, and forty-three dikes were integrated into the structure. The completed reservoir, when filled in 1981, contained enough water to service a city the size of Montréal for almost a century.

Happily, even after this magnificent achievement, the original state of the land was not forgotten. Construction sites were filled in, and new trees and shrubs were planted. There are plans for the eventual planting of four million seedlings and saplings.

A Mighty River Harnessed

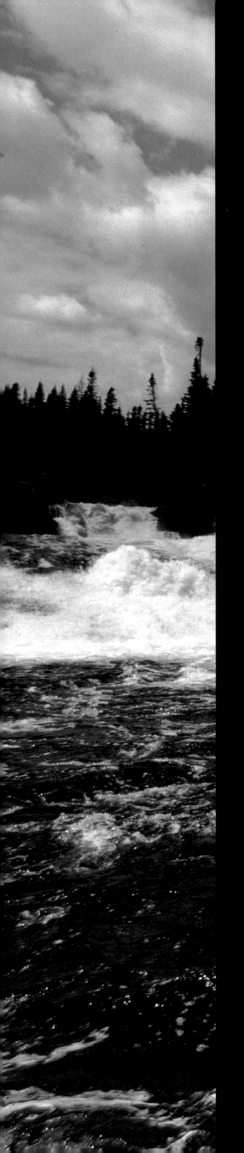

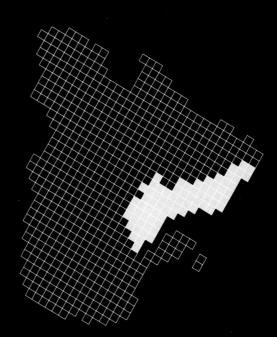

In the last century, this vast, forested, lake-riddled wilderness on the north shore of the St. Lawrence was known only to Indians and occasional fishermen and trappers. These venturers never dreamed—and perhaps never cared to dream—of the huge reserves of mineral wealth that lay beneath their feet, in such present-day settlements as Sept-Iles, Port-Cartier and Clarke City.

From the 1930s onward, the region's vast resources of iron ore, wood and water were heavily exploited. Rapid development accompanied this change of pace. Mines and factories sprang up, and communities grew swiftly around them. With the economic recession of the 1980s, however, the demand for iron ore diminished drastically.

The north shore today is adjusting to a new and challenging vocation: tourism. During its short but exhilarating summer, thrilling canoe-camping experiences and excellent fishing opportunities await those who penetrate this wild, sparsely populated frontier—a region little changed from yesteryear.

The North Shore

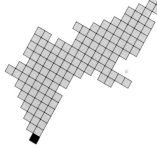

TADOUSSAC

Tadoussac (*above*), a rugged perch overlooking the ancient Saguenay. The first European known to have landed here was Jacques Cartier, in 1535. A cross erected 400 years later beside the Tadoussac Church commemorates this event.

Twilight spreads across the waters of the Saguenay (*right*) revealing the specter of a ship heading into port. Ghostly overtones aside, the vessel is most likely returning from a successful day of whale-sighting in the nearby St. Lawrence.

Set high atop sandy cliffs at the mouth of the Saguenay River, Tadoussac occupies a realm all of its own—neither part of the north shore nor of Charlevoix County. The homes and summer cottages of its thousand or so inhabitants are barely visible among the surrounding dunes, yet this village is well known, and has been for more than three centuries.

Tadoussac—a Montagnais word for hillock—was one of North America's first European settlements. A cross erected here in 1935 commemorates Jacques Cartier's exploration of the area 400 years earlier. In 1600 Pierre Chauvin, who had been granted a ten-year fur-trade monopoly, chose this site for his headquarters. His fortified house—Canada's first trading post—became the center of a thriving business, bartering close to 25,000 furs in 1648 alone. A replica of that stockade stands on what is believed to be the original site.

In 1747, Father Godefroy Coquart, a missionary who spent almost two decades with the Montagnais Indians, built what is today North America's oldest surviving chapel. When he died in 1765, his remains were interred within. The chapel bell, dating to 1641, was salvaged from a Jesuit church that once stood on this same spot.

People continue to flock to Tadoussac each summer, but now many bring skis instead of pelts. Wearing shorts and heavy boots, they climb the 550 steps to the top of a steep sand dune, where they don skis, and enjoy an exhilarating schuss to the bottom. Sand skiing is the name of this unusual activity.

Tadoussac's dunes flank a broad, natural harbor, once a favorite port of call for ships such as the *Bonne Renommée*, which arrived on May 26, 1603, carrying Samuel de Champlain on his first voyage to Canada. Basque mariners also docked regularly at the port in those days, trading whale oil for furs.

In the Footsteps of Cartier

THE NORTH SHORE

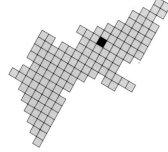

MANIC 5

Two faces of Manic 5 (*above* and *right*), both showing the arch-and-buttress style of construction that characterizes the Daniel Johnson Dam. Multiple-arch dams of this type are able to withstand enormous water pressures because of support columns, or buttresses, rooted in the bedrock at the base of the retaining wall. (Conventional dams depend only on their own weight to resist water pressure.) The dam is located one kilometre upstream from the powerhouse.

Manic 5 is one of the biggest and most photographed hydroelectric installations in the world. It attracts more than 80,000 sightseers a year and is the unchallenged highlight of any visit to the Manicouagan River basin.

The project began in 1959, and the plant was put into full operation 11 years later. Now, at peak output, Manic 5's eight huge generators combined can produce some 1,292,000 kilowatts—enough electricity to illuminate more than two million 60-watt lightbulbs.

Manic 5 is fed by a 2000-square-kilometre reservoir, the most expansive in the entire Manic-Outardes hydroelectric project. The water is maintained at a level of 154 metres and held in check by the Daniel Johnson Dam, the largest arch-and-buttress dam in the world. Passageways within the wall of the dam contain various hair-trigger mechanisms which monitor the slightest movement in the structure and detect any fluctuations in its internal stresses.

Water from the reservoir is conducted to the turbines by means of intake tunnels, 11 metres in diameter. Two vertical surge tanks absorb the enormous increase in pressure that occurs the moment the intake valves are clamped shut.

Hydro-Québec is presently constructing a new underground powerhouse opposite the existing one. This installation will increase the present electrical output by almost 80 percent, and is scheduled for completion in 1989. Both powerhouses will be used, together, at times of the year when demand for electricity in the province is at its highest.

A Modern Riverside Colossus

THE NORTH SHORE

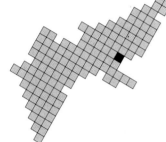

SEPT-ILES

History and tradition make fishing more than just a livelihood in the Sept-Iles area (*above* and *right*). Since Jacques Cartier first anchored here in the 1530s, the practice of taking fish from the sea has been an ongoing one. The original Indian inhabitants were fishermen, as were many of the white settlers who followed later. And even with the recent boom times that accompanied Sept-Iles' increased importance as an iron ore transportation center, the occupation still endures.

Sept-Iles is a bustling north shore shipping port on the rim of an almost circular bay. Recognized for its deepwater harbor as far back as the time of Jacques Cartier, the present-day city was named for what appear to be seven rocky atolls near the entrance to the bay. (There are actually only six islands—the "seventh" is part of the mainland.)

Sept-Iles originated as a fishing and fur trade community, inhabited primarily by Indians. In 1866 the township of Letellier was established, and settlers followed gradually. But even by 1950, Sept-Iles was still a fishing village with a population of only 1,500 inhabitants. With the post-World War II demand for steel in the United States, however, the vast iron ore deposits of Schefferville began to be exploited in earnest, and Sept-Iles' emerging importance as a shipping center quickly became apparent.

A 600-kilometre-long railway—using remote-controlled trains—was built to haul iron ore from the mines of Schefferville, Labrador City, and Wabush, and it was soon found that some 10 million tonnes of ore could be loaded in one six-month shipping season. With this sudden prosperity, the population of Sept-Iles swelled to 30,000.

Sept-Iles is still the commercial and administrative hub of the north shore, linked to other major Québec communities by regular airline service. It sits firmly at the edge of a resource-rich wilderness and offers a wealth of unexplored forests and unfished lakes to adventurous vacationers. One of the areas most popular with outdoor enthusiasts lies just west of the city, the vast Réserve Port-Cartier–Sept-Iles.

A North Shore Ore Town

THE NORTH SHORE

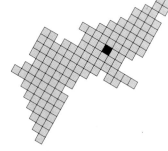

MOISIE

Remote as it is, the north shore attracts its share of tourists— and often surprises first-time visitors with the quality of its charms. *Above*: a popular swimming beach at Moisie.

Such idyllic beauty (*right*) may long ago have witnessed the bartering of fur traders and local Indians, birchbarks pulled onto the sand, and hefty pelts piled on the beach. Although the traders are no more, the wilderness remains as quiet and unspoiled as ever.

The Moisie is a deep, swift-currented, and only partially navigable river. Rapids, waterfalls, and arduous portages punctuate its tumultuous 304-kilometre descent from the interior of the north shore to the Gulf of St. Lawrence. Yet, difficult as it is to negotiate, this was one of the most frequented of the Gulf tributaries during the fur trade era. It flowed through a region thick with game, and each spring Indians and trappers met with fur traders on the sandy banks of the river's estuary to barter. Today the Moisie is still one of the best salmon rivers in eastern North America; an abundance of sea trout are also found in its waters.

The village of Moisie is a very old settlement situated just west of the river. Europeans first arrived here in 1688, and some years later the Hudson's Bay Company established a trading post. Little more occurred in the area, however, until about 1860, when a group of colonists decided to settle permanently. They soon discovered iron ore deposits along the river, and for a decade or so Moisie flickered briefly as a mining community.

Out of this short-lived success, a neighboring community— aptly named Forges—was born. This town has since fallen to ruin, but just over a hundred years ago it was the center of a prosperous ironworks, supplying clients in the United States. With the unanticipated passage of duty laws, however, the mining came to an abrupt halt.

Today, heavy industry is noticeably a thing of the past. The Department of Recreation, Fish and Game maintains a large campground at the mouth of the Moisie, and canoeists and fishing enthusiasts come here regularly to test their skills on the rapids and enjoy the area's fine fishing.

Artery of the Fur Trade

154

THE NORTH SHORE

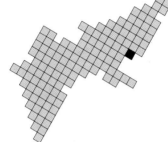

RIVIERE-AU-TONNERRE

Seabirds and fishing boats
(*above*), the early-morning
charms of Rivière-au-Tonnerre.
Such tranquility of scenery
seems strangely at odds with
the hamlet's name—translated,
Rivière-au-Tonnerre means
"Thunder River."

Waiting for a congregation that
never showed up (*right*),
Rivière-au-Tonnerre's oversized
church looks stalwartly out onto
a shoreline that for centuries
has discouraged settlement.

Rivière-au-Tonnerre, 120 kilometres east of Sept-Iles, is typical of the colorful surprises that lie along the brooding north shore of the St. Lawrence. A region blessed with neither rich soil, nor an inviting climate, it is, as Jacques Cartier once remarked, "The land God gave to Cain." Yet despite this admonition, Rivière-au-Tonnerre is a small and cheerfully thriving Québécois fishing hamlet with a population of some 600 inhabitants.

Long before the first French settlers arrived in North America, Basque fishermen were defying the low forbidding cliffs and inhospitable shores of this region in order to take advantage of the abundant fish in the area. The beaches were then—as now—strewn with large boulders gouged from the landscape by powerful tides and ice, and the countryside offered few trees to relieve the bleak horizon. It was an area that would have to wait long for permanent settlement.

Rivière-au-Tonnerre's first chapel was erected in 1875, when only a handful of families lived here. This chapel was soon replaced by a larger and more elaborate structure whose seating capacity far exceeded the needs of the community; the builders had anticipated a population increase that never came to pass.

Facing the sea, and adorned with panels and sculptures lovingly carved out of wood by parishioners, the present-day church survives as a splendid example of north shore ecclesiastic architecture—a testament to the indispensable faith of the early fishermen who settled this remote corner of Québec.

The Land God Gave to Cain

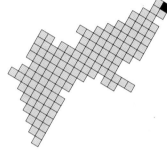

MINGAN

Crumbling shale formations (*above*) give shape to much of the craggy Mingan coastline, one of the wildest regions on the continent.

Oversized gargoyles (*right*): a scene typical of the Mingan archipelago. "Islands" here range from solitary rocky pedestals, such as those in the photograph, to larger, habitable patches of land. But settlement throughout the region is lean.

Just across from the western tip of Anticosti Island in the Gulf of St. Lawrence, the north shore coastline fractures into a cluster of islets known as the Mingan archipelago. There are some fifty islets in all, many of them uninhabited, for this region is one of the wildest and remotest in North America. To get there, motorists must follow Highway 138, a solitary but scenic coastal route that winds eastward from Sept-Iles, some 200 kilometres distant.

Mingan, the unofficial capital of this region, is a quiet north shore village looking out onto the archipelago. Like many other mainland ports in this area, it is protected from the strong gulf tides by natural breakwaters. During the 1700s the village was a busy trading and fishing post. Before that Basque whalers plied its waters.

Today Mingan is little more than a gentle refuge for travelers seeking true seclusion. The wilderness here is awesome, and summers—although fleeting—are lovely. From late June through August, a tourist information center in the village directs visitors to local accommodations and attractions. There are several ancient archeological sites in the area.

Beyond Mingan, Highway 138 continues on to Havre St-Pierre, some 40 kilometres east. From there on, the remaining handful of isolated hamlets are connected by a primitive riverfront road. These hardy settlements rely mainly on coastal vessels and bush planes for any contact with the outside world.

A Gentle Refuge in the Wilds

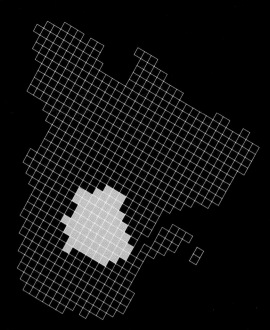

These twin regions cover an immense territory which Jacques Cartier once dubbed the "Saguenay Kingdom." This title, however, has since become figurative: residents today know this vast tract of land as two distinct regions—one industrial and one agricultural—both closely linked economically.

The Saguenay region, with its aluminum and pulp-and-paper resources, has become industrialized and its population is mostly urban. The Lac-St-Jean region depends largely on farming and forestry. The lake itself, an almost circular basin with a perimeter of 225 kilometres, is fed by more than a dozen rivers. It provides some of the province's best fishing for landlocked salmon, and is blessed with a wealth of sparkling waterfalls and a number of lovely lakeside recreation areas.

A journey through this fascinating realm and around its beautiful big lake, it has often been said, is a little like a fairy tale. Slightly dreamy, slightly nostalgic—above all, an invitation to discovery.

Saguenay/ Lac-St-Jean

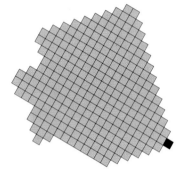

L'ANSE-ST-JEAN

L'Anse-St-Jean (*above*), seemingly in miniature. An image that speaks of Christmas and the joys of the simple life. In the background, the snow-clad Laurentians—ancient hills that cradle some 700 rivers and twice as many lakes.

A solitary fishing boat rests at anchor in the bay beside L'Anse-St-Jean (*right*). Since the village's founding in 1838, residents—as is customary throughout the Saguenay and Charlevoix regions—have traditionally spent part of each year harvesting a livelihood from the rich local fishing grounds.

L'Anse-St-Jean is a quiet, old-world village 80 kilometres east of Chicoutimi. Resting on the edge of a tranquil bay where the Rivière St-Jean flows into the mighty Saguenay, the settlement dates to the late 1830s. Yet even today there are scarcely more than 1,500 residents in the entire community, most of them descendants of the original colonists.

The village is typical of the farming and lumber communities that sprang up throughout this region in the last century. However, after a brief flirtation with agriculture, L'Anse-St-Jean devoted itself primarily to producing finely fashioned rowboats and handsomely constructed schooners. These craft were once a common sight on the Saguenay, when lumber was shipped downriver to Québec City and Trois-Rivières.

A nostalgic throwback to those times is the old single-lane covered bridge spanning the Rivière St-Jean, one of the last structures of its kind in the Saguenay region. Farther along the riverbank, picnic areas and scenic lookouts adjoin graceful waterfalls.

Today, L'Anse-St-Jean straddles both past and present—with tourism the newest ingredient in the village's economy. A large, well-equipped nautical park attracts many vacationers throughout summer. Camping, sailing, and excellent fishing for trout and salmon are the principal attractions. Visitors can also stay at the Nazaire Boudreault Farm on the outskirts of the village. Old-time farming methods are practiced here, with little use of machinery and a shunning of pesticides. Not far from the farm, a hiking trail winds to the top of Cap Trinité and a spectacular view of the ancient Saguenay.

A Step Away From Yesterday

SAGUENAY/LAC-ST-JEAN

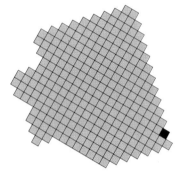

CAP TRINITE

A view of the Rivière Eternité (*above*): a remote and primitive landscape endowed with a special kind of allure. Even the names of the twin peaks— "Trinity" and "Eternity"—that flank the entrance to this river seem to speak of mystery.

Cap Trinité (*right*), a wall of stone challenged by only the most intrepid of climbers. The base of the rock begins some 240 metres underwater.

Two towering and formidable sentinels of rock—Cap Trinité and Cap Eternité—guard the entrance to the Rivière Eternité, midway between Chicoutimi and Baie-Ste-Catherine, on the south shore of the Saguenay River. Both of these granite cliffs are located within Saguenay Provincial Park. The cold and murky waters at their base span almost two kilometres, a prospect that adds nothing, if not a forbidding quality, to this brooding corner of the province.

Nonetheless, Cap Trinité's vertical wall lures both climbing enthusiasts and sightseers with its awesome sheerness. Generations of climbers have worn flat the sparse patches of vegetation that pock the cliff face, and passengers crowd the rails of passing cruise boats for a good view of this natural colossus.

An eight-metre-high statue of the Virgin Mary tops Cap Trinité's summit. Sculpted out of rough-hewn wood coated with lead, the Madonna has overlooked the Saguenay since 1881, when it was hoisted to its perilous perch with ropes and winches, an act of faith in itself.

A gravel trail just off Route 170, on the outskirts of L'Anse-St-Jean, winds to the 500-metre-high pinnacle. From here a magnificent viewpoint gives onto the Baie Eternité and the dark, surging, amber-colored waters of the Saguenay.

Within Saguenay Provincial Park, a nature interpretation center remains open to visitors throughout the summer. Guided tours of Cap Eternité and the surrounding landscape can be arranged through this office.

A Prospect of the Saguenay

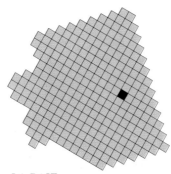

LA BAIE

Storm clouds gather over the Baie des Ha! Ha! (*above*). No one really knows how the bay came to be named, but one theory is that Ha! Ha! derives from an Indian word for something unexpected, as in a pleasant surprise.

Set on the gentle banks of the Rivière-à-Mars (*right*), La Baie maintains a fine balance between the beauty of the surrounding landscape and the inroads made by industrialization.

La Baie is an amalgamation of three neighboring townships facing the strange-named Baie des Ha! Ha! on the Saguenay. Its deep harbor, sheltered by massive rocky escarpments jutting from the Saguenay's north shore, has made it a major stopping-off point for generations of mariners. Nowadays some 500 freighters dock annually at La Baie to unload bauxite destined for aluminum smelters in Arvida, and to take on newsprint manufactured in local paper mills.

La Baie's three municipalities—Bagotville, Port Alfred, and Grande Baie—range along a small valley drained by the Rivière-à-Mars. This was one of the first areas to be colonized, and it was considered the cradle of civilization in Jacques Cartier's "Saguenay Kingdom." The earliest settlers arrived in 1838, from the Baie St-Paul area. They hacked a community from the richly wooded countryside and constructed lumber mills to process the vast local timber reserves. Carpentry shops, where craftsmen fashioned ship parts, sprang up alongside the mills. Today La Baie's 23,000 inhabitants rely mainly on the Alcan aluminum company and on the Consolidated Bathurst factory for their livelihood.

One of the main objectives of this community has been to maintain harmony between the town's industrial development and its natural surroundings. The results are appealing. A lovely park, with Florentine-style landscaping, overlooks the majestic Saguenay fjord. Picturesque Mars Park, nearby, also makes a significant contribution to the area's beauty. One of its highlights is an ornithological center where about 50 species of aquatic birds can be observed.

In remembrance of La Baie's beginnings, the townspeople organize a lively festival each year toward mid-June to reenact the rigorous epic of the pioneers.

'Throne' of Cartier's Kingdom

SAGUENAY/LAC-ST-JEAN

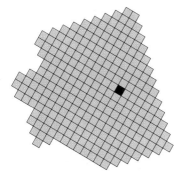

CHICOUTIMI

A captivated audience (*above*), enthralled by a clownish exchange at Chicoutimi's Carnaval-Souvenir (Carnival of Memories). During this festive period, many of the residents wear colorful costumes both at home and at work—as well as in the streets.

Chicoutimi (*right*), a city with staying power. Here the snows of winter serve only to fuel the community's pride—in its past, its present, and its ability to prevail in a land that grants few favors.

Chicoutimi, a bustling inland seaport 210 kilometres north of Québec City, is the Saguenay region's metropolis. It stands on the hilly south shore of the Saguenay River, flanked to the east and west by the Chicoutimi and du Moulin rivers. Directly south of Chicoutimi and the neighboring town of Jonquière sprawls the vast and forested wilderness of Réserve faunique des Laurentides.

In its early days, the mid-1800s, Chicoutimi was a hardy community of barely 1,400 inhabitants who made their livings either at Peter McLeod's sawmill or by way of river commerce during the summer months. Today the city breathes an air of prosperity, with such distinctions as a modern hospital complex and several widely respected educational establishments.

Nonetheless, pioneer roots are not forgotten in Chicoutimi, for residents are justly proud of their rugged past. During an eight-day Carnaval-Souvenir each year, they fondly commemorate the settling of this winter-ravaged land. The festival takes place just before Lent, when the snowbound city revels in the sights and sounds of wood-chopping contests, snowshoe races, tugs-of-war, and torchlight parades and dances. Many of the 35,000 residents wear period costume. Further traces of Chicoutimi's cherished past can be glimpsed at the Saguenay Museum, where a gold watch and other memorabilia belonging to Peter McLeod are among the many exhibits displayed.

From the Chicoutimi waterfront visitors can take eight-hour Saguenay cruises to Cap Trinité and Cap Eternité, and four-hour trips to Ste-Rose-du-Nord.

History Relived by Torchlight

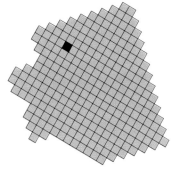

MISTASSINI

Rock-strewn rivers surge throughout the Mistassini region (*above*), feeding into vast Lac St-Jean. This almost circular lake covers an area of more than 1000 square kilometres and is an age-old glacial trough that was once an arm of the sea.

About 25 percent of the nearly 13,000 tonnes of blueberries harvested annually in Canada come from Québec. Mistassini, with its lucrative yield, is the province's greatest producer of these berries (*right*).

Blueberries are Canada's most valuable native fruit—and they grow in such quantities throughout Mistassini that this small town is known as the blueberry capital of Québec. The fields of this area abound with wild blueberries, as well as with cultured varieties, which are grown for export.

Mistassini celebrates the ripening of its prized crop with an annual mid-August blueberry festival. Visitors can pick their own berries from those growing wild in the fields, or buy them freshly packed at local fruit stalls. Farm-baked blueberry pies, jars of blueberry jam, and even bottles of blueberry wine are sold. Indeed, wine tasting is one of the most popular features of the festival.

The Mistassini Valley lies between two natural barriers: huge granite outcroppings and glacial debris the height of three-story buildings (to which Indians long ago gave the name Mistassini—meaning "large boulders"); and vast, dense forestland. Domtar took advantage of this expansive wilderness and built a paper factory on the Mistassini River in 1927. Logging soon became an important business. These industries, coupled with the construction of three hydroelectric dams on the Péribonka River 20 years later, contributed considerably to the area's industrial importance.

In 1892, when Mistassini was still a wilderness, Trappist monks built a monastery on the banks of the Mistassini River. They also cleared a large section of forest for farmland and opened up a chocolate factory. The monastery was converted into an abbey in 1935. The huge Trappist farm, however, continues to produce crops to this day.

Québec's Blueberry Belt

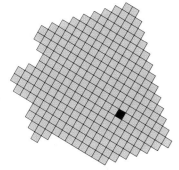

RESERVE FAUNIQUE DES LAURENTIDES

Réserve faunique des Lauren-tides (*above*): untrammeled, fir-clad wilderness—and enough space for anyone to find peace and solitude for an hour, a day, or weeks on end.

In Réserve faunique des Laurentides all animals—with the exception of moose and fish—are protected (*right*). The result is a spectacular wilderness that everyone can enjoy.

In 1895, following the success of a U.S. nature conservation movement that designed Yellowstone National Park, the Québec government set aside 8000 square kilometres of land between Québec City and Lac St-Jean to become "Parc National des Laurentides." Today this lovely sanctuary— now named Réserve faunique des Laurentides—preserves the natural beauty of this pristine landscape, as well as the area's abundant animal life.

A major section of the park was designated a wildlife reserve in 1981. It thus became the fourth largest in the province after Chibougamau, Mistassini, and La Vérendrye. This specially recognized area was created in order to protect such native creatures as moose, beaver, otter, black bear, wolf, and red fox.

Nowadays fishermen, canoeists, boaters, hikers, and camping enthusiasts all partake of the park's wooded hillsides, green meadows, and numerous lakes and streams. Moose are the only animals that may be hunted, and licenses are limited. (Hunters must register in advance, then participate in a drawing.) Several of the local rivers are prized for their speckled trout. The park also provides boats for visitors seeking to navigate the lakes, including some of the larger bodies of water—Lac Jacques-Cartier, Lac aux Ecorces, and Lac des Neiges.

Facilities within this vast nature retreat are many and varied. Cottages, as well as a colorfully named lodge—the "Portes de l'Enfer" (Gates of Hell)—enable anglers to enjoy a few relaxing days fishing the area's bountiful waterways. Cabins are also available during winter for vacationers wishing to snowshoe or ski cross-country.

A Century-Old Sanctuary

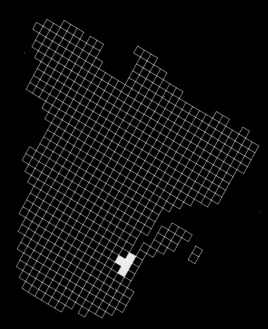

Charlevoix County stretches along the north shore of the St. Lawrence from Baie-St-Paul to the Saguenay Estuary. This rich and unusually beautiful tapestry of green river valleys, rugged hills and craggy coastline is one of Québec's most alluring vacation regions, located a mere 100 kilometres east of Québec City.

Old farming and fishing communities—many dating to the end of the 17th century—are found throughout. The majority of early residents came from the nearby Beaupré coast, settling initially along the fertile coastline, then moving gradually inland.

To offset its diminishing agricultural and forest industries Charlevoix depends on a vigorous tourist trade. (Pointe-au-Pic and La Malbaie, two of North America's oldest resort towns, have drawn significant numbers of visitors since the late 1800s.) The region also has a highly successful arts and crafts industry. But its greatest resource, by far, is the splendor of its countryside.

Charlevoix

CHARLEVOIX

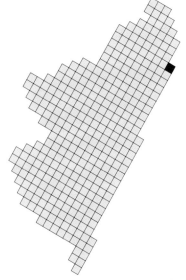

ST-SIMEON

St-Siméon (*right*): a welcoming bay for ferry passengers from the south shore. Here Highway 138 turns inland, climbs the Laurentians and brushes past sparkling lakes and dense forests of cedar and white birch. Travelers in late July may chance upon the town's annual smelt festival, and roadside stands offering fresh-caught fish.

Each year, around mid-July, vast silvery waves of tiny fish roll in toward St-Siméon, a lovely shoreline village 185 kilometres east of Québec City. These salmon-like miniatures—called smelt—work their way up the St. Lawrence to spawn. In the mild July evenings, clusters of fishermen gather on the quay, flashlights in hand, eager to harvest this annual gift from the sea. It is then that St-Siméon earns its title as "smelt capital" of Charlevoix. As might be expected, these tasty fish are a favorite regional dish, served in many of the area's restaurants and inns.

In days gone by, St-Siméon was a busy and vital port, when handsome schooners carried cargoes of wood, farm produce and manufactured goods upriver and even down to Newfoundland. Today, the schooners are mere memories and St-Siméon now depends on the forest industry for much of its livelihood. Nonetheless, with a ferry linking Rivière-du-Loup and St-Siméon, the village is still one of the most traveled-through spots in this part of Charlevoix. From the wharf, a hilly road winds on through to La Baie and Chicoutimi.

There is excellent fishing—for speckled trout and salmon—in the shaded streams and hidden lakes surrounding St-Siméon. Little more than a dozen kilometres northwest of the village, Les Palissades, a nature study center operated by the Québec Ministry of Energy and Resources, is crisscrossed by hiking trails. Here, nature enthusiasts can learn about the geology of the region. A dozen kilometres southwest, another nature center, at Port-au-Saumon, is known for its wealth of aquatic flora.

A Summer Gift from the Sea

CHARLEVOIX

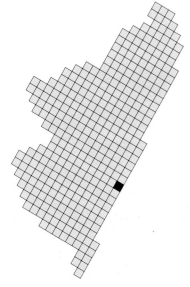

LES EBOULEMENTS

A realm of magnificent greenery—the very essence of the Charlevoix region (*above*)— surrounds Les Eboulements. It is hard to imagine that such a countryside could ever have suffered an earthquake or landslide. Yet in 1663, when the first of a series of devastating quakes occurred, frightened Indians believed that "the streams were full of firewater and the forests were drunk."

The De Sales-Laterrière Mill (*right*), one of two handsomely preserved watermills in Les Eboulements. The seigneurial manor, dating to the last century, stands nearby.

One hundred and twenty kilometres east of Québec City, in the heart of Charlevoix county, lies Les Eboulements, a village set amid a luxuriant forest plateau cut by deep gorges and narrow valleys. Throughout this area, old rustic roads wind through a countryside which has always been less than fertile, but which nonetheless has been obstinately cultivated by generations of determined farmers. Perhaps just as impervious to the environment are the gray, weatherbeaten farmhouses built by the first settlers of the region.

Les Eboulements' dramatic locale overlooking the St. Lawrence makes it almost irresistible to painters and tourists. At one time the village crouched closer to a cliff, but two massive landslides (the last one, around 1830) radically altered its topography. Nowadays, because of these earth shifts, an awesome view of the St. Lawrence fans out from the church square, some 350 metres above the river.

The church itself, Notre-Dame-de-l'Assomption, is one of the region's most handsome. It was reconstructed in 1932, after fire destroyed the original. Exquisite examples of ecclesiastical sculpture and woodwork lie within. One such work, retrieved from the fire, is the remains of an ornate altar shelf, meticulously carved by François Baillargé in 1775.

The nearby De Sales-Laterrière Manor and its mill and adjoining buildings date to Les Eboulements' second seigneury, in the 19th century. (The first seigneury was located farther back from the river, at a time when the shoreline was deeper.) Today these historic structures are owned by the Brothers of the Sacred Heart. Another local mill, at the edge of a waterfall overlooking a stream, dates back more than 180 years. It was acquired by the Canadian Heritage Society in the early 1960s.

A View Left by a Landslide

CHARLEVOIX

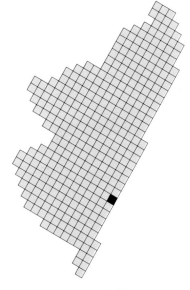

ILE AUX COUDRES

Quaint windmills, historic
chapels, and centuries-old
dwellings dot the landscape
throughout Ile aux Coudres
(*above*).

The north shore (*right*), from a
hillside on Ile aux Coudres. A
living miniature of 18th-
century France, the entire
island measures no more than
11 kilometres by 3, and
supports four small
communities.

Hazelnut trees grew in abundance during the early 16th
century on this small island off the north shore of the St.
Lawrence. Thus when Jacques Cartier landed here on
September 7, 1535, he christened the place—in the language
of his time—in acknowledgment of them. Four hundred and
fifty years later, Ile aux Coudres carries the distinction of
being the place where Mass was first celebrated in Canada, the
day of Cartier's arrival. A large granite cross in St-Bernard-sur-
Mer commemorates the event.

Colonists from Baie-St-Paul received Ile aux Coudres' first
land grants in 1728. These hardy settlers constructed quaint
stone houses with metre-thick walls and erected picturesque
windmills, which today look as solid as when they were built.
Present-day visitors to Ile aux Coudres are left with the almost-
tangible impression that they have stepped back into a sleepy
province in 18th-century France.

Until the 1960s, Ile aux Coudres was cut off from the
mainland throughout winter because of slab-ice that formed in
the river. Today, a modern ferry operates year-round, several
times a day, transporting cars and pedestrians to St-Joseph-de-
la-Rive, 15 minutes away.

Once a little-known and virtually isolated fishing
community, Ile aux Coudres is now quickly becoming popular
as an idyllic vacation spot. To accommodate the soaring
number of tourists each year, many of the ancient, thick-walled
buildings have been converted into small inns and charming
hotels furnished with period pieces. One of the island's favorite
tourist attractions, however, has little to do with history.
La Maison Croche (the Crooked House) dates only to 1963.
It stands at La Baleine on the northeastern tip of Ile aux
Coudres, and is a unique, topsy-turvy architectural curiosity.
It is open to the public.

Where Time Stands Still

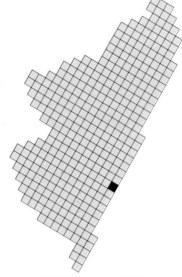

ST-JOSEPH-DE-LA-RIVE

Harmony of line, angle, and open space: a study in rural symmetry (*above*). This farm is on the outskirts of St-Joseph-de-la-Rive.

Tucked away from the rest of the world, tiny St-Joseph-de-la-Rive (*right*), recluse of the north shore. A solitary main road connects it with the highway—Route 362—and Les Eboulements, four kilometres northeast.

High cliffs hide it from the world, and the St. Lawrence sweeps on by it, and even time itself seems at a remove from tiny St-Joseph-de-la-Rive. Yet in its heyday, the late 1800s and early 1900s, this secluded fieldstone village was one of the busiest shipbuilding ports in this area of the north shore.

At its peak, St-Joseph saw the construction of nearly 80 large seagoing vessels, many of which became supply ships up and down the St. Lawrence and to points beyond. Village shipwrights, who were often skilled navigators, maintained a closely guarded tradition of craftsmanship. Today many of these techniques are lost to the past, and the boatyard is all but silent. Only a handful of villagers continue to make their livings from shipbuilding, mostly by constructing or repairing fishing and pleasure boats.

In recent times, St-Joseph has become known for the deluxe, hand-crafted paper produced at La Papeterie Saint-Gilles. Bowing to tradition, this local paper mill uses machines only for tasks that cannot be performed manually. Visitors are invited to watch the fascinating process as rag-fiber, maple leaves, wildflowers and ferns are combined with pastes and dyes and sifted in a large vat. The mixture is then shaped, pressed on blotters, hung on lines to dry, and fed between steel rollers. The end product is a smooth, filigreed parchment in tones of white, blue and green bearing the distinctive watermark effigy of Saint Gilles.

A World Away From the World

CHARLEVOIX

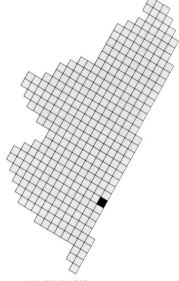

BAIE-ST-PAUL

Surely one of the prettiest towns in the entire province, Baie-St-Paul (*above*) has long seduced anyone with an eye for the picturesque.

A hazy day on the outskirts of Baie-St-Paul (*right*). Aside from natural beauty, the countryside in this area is blessed with an abundance of wildlife— including bear, hare, moose and partridge. Anglers can fish for arctic char and speckled trout.

Few places in Québec can match the natural charms of Baie-St-Paul. Nestled between two promontories at the mouth of the Rivière du Gouffre, 100 kilometres east of Québec City, this town of barely 5,000 inhabitants is widely regarded as being one of the most picturesque spots in the entire province. The stately St. Lawrence winds past in the distance, and green Laurentian hills gaze down upon it, taking in the town's narrow streets and fieldstone houses, its solitary church spire and gentle bay beyond.

Baie-St-Paul is endowed with a number of handsome buildings. The Franciscan Convent and the Hospice of Saint Anne are fine examples of traditional architecture rich in rural character. The town church, at the center of Baie-St-Paul, dates to 1907. It was ravaged by fire in 1967, and has now had its interior handsomely refurbished. Other notable structures in the area are the two French-period gristmills, the Michel Perron and La Rémy mills, which still operate. The César mill, which dates to 1722, is today an art gallery.

Over the years, Baie-St-Paul's lovely setting has attracted artists by the score. They come to paint and photograph the area's fertile fields, its bold hills, its weathered farms and quaint town houses. Canvases depicting the area hang in museums and private collections throughout the country. Indeed, among Québec places, only Montréal and Québec City appear more often in the National Gallery of Canada. Perhaps the most famous of all Baie-St-Paul artists was Clarence Gagnon (1881-1942). Gagnon spent his last years here, capturing on canvas this quintessential Québec town, and confirming its reputation as a place of truly timeless beauty.

Picture-Perfect, by the Bay

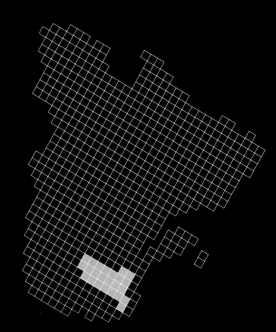

The old "Chemin du Roy," built in 1734, was the first carriageway to link Montréal with Québec City. The road now follows the meandering course of the St. Lawrence River, passing through numerous towns and villages before ending up in Ste-Anne-de-Beaupré.

This venerable thoroughfare witnessed a varied and continuous stream of history, as armies, explorers and colonists made their way down its beaten track. Today, echoes of this past greet travelers at almost every turn: manors, old churches and traditional fieldstone houses line its route.

Trois-Rivières, in Québec's heartland, has been a popular stopping-off point since its founding in 1634. Located at the churning confluence of the St-Maurice and St. Lawrence rivers, this industrial town is also one of the province's most historic. Museums, monuments, and several early buildings attest to its status as Canada's second oldest city after Québec.

Some 115 kilometres to the east of Trois-Rivières, past the tiny and picturesque communities of Batiscan, Deschambault and Portneuf, lies Québec City itself. Perched atop a huge rock promontory overlooking the river, this "Grande Dame" of French Canada is one of our continent's most photographed cities.

Québec, La Mauricie, Bois-Francs

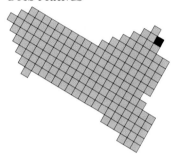

ST-FERREOL-LES-NEIGES

St-Ferréol-les-Neiges (*right*),
gateway to lovely Parc du Mont-
Ste-Anne. Popular with
outdoors enthusiasts of all ages,
this rugged resort area abounds
with rivers, waterfalls, and
dense stands of yellow birch.

St-Ferréol's enviable location on the outskirts of Parc du Mont-Ste-Anne—one of eastern Canada's prime recreation areas—has no doubt contributed to the hamlet's popularity as a holiday resort in recent years. But St-Ferréol exerts other charms as well. A short distance upstream from here, the Rivière Ste-Anne-du-Nord cascades 125 metres over Les Sept Chutes, a series of cataracts, before it bubbles past the village and its many handsomely restored homes. The village church, an 1842 reconstruction of an earlier chapel, dominates the tiny community. Just northeast of here, one can tour the piscicultural station of Aulnais-sous-Bois, and nearby, a federal seismological laboratory.

But most visitors to St-Ferréol come for the park and its array of outdoor facilities. Parc du Mont-Ste-Anne lures a variety of pleasure-seekers, no matter what time of year, with breathtaking downhill ski slopes, some 175 kilometres of cross-country ski and snowshoe trails, a network of bicycle paths, and numerous campgrounds. Gondolas climb to the top of Mont-Ste-Anne, more than 800 metres high, and a splendid vista of the surrounding landscape.

This corner of the Beaupré Coast, 48 kilometres east of Québec, was first explored in 1693 by Canon Soumandre of the Québec Seminary. He led deer hunting parties into the woods which are now part of the park. But, although the Canon vaunted the scenic glories and rich wildlife of this region to his bishop, colonization did not begin until 1728.

Historians today can only speculate on how St-Ferréol received its name. One theory claims it originated with a superior of the Québec Seminary who once controlled the Beaupré seigneury. The more likely theory is that it was named after the mountain town of St-Ferréol in southern France.

A Place for All Seasons

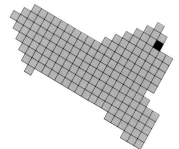

CAP-TOURMENTE

Blue sky for a roof, and wind in the doorway (*above*): the ruins of Maison de la Brie, at Cap-Tourmente, not far from the spot where Champlain grazed cattle almost 370 years ago.

Hundreds of thousands of snow geese—migrating between breeding grounds on Baffin Island and wintering grounds in Virginia and North Carolina—make Cap-Tourmente a bird watcher's delight (*right*).

Since 1969, Cap-Tourmente has been the site of a national wildlife reserve created to protect the natural habitat of snow geese. There were fewer than 5,000 of these birds at the turn of the century but today, because of the sanctuary, their numbers have increased to approximately 200,000.

Located near the village of St-Joachim, about 45 kilometres east of Québec City, the reserve stands on land that was once part of a vast seigneurial estate. La Petite Ferme, a historic building in St-Joachim, maintains a reception center for tourists visiting the wildlife park.

For six weeks during spring and autumn Cap-Tourmente is virtually buried under flurries of snow geese. The birds arrive by the thousands, alighting on the surrounding fields and pastures before settling along the broad shoreline of the reserve. Their numbers are greatest during the month of October, when they return from summer nesting grounds on the arctic islands.

Observing wildlife on Cap-Tourmente is a popular pastime for visitors. A winding trail leads to a clifftop where spectators can look out over the bird-dappled waters of the St. Lawrence and across to Ile d'Orléans and the south shore. As well as snow geese, there are more than 20 other species of birds within the sanctuary. These include ducks, Canada geese, herons, swallows, warblers, and teals.

An interpretive center focuses on the life history and habitats of snow geese and local songbirds. Naturalists conduct walks through the sanctuary, and a pathway leads to the summit of the cape.

Domain of the Snow Goose

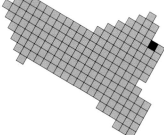

MONTMORENCY FALLS

The "sugarloaf" at Montmorency Falls (*above*). In the last century revelers sleighed down the cone and fought off winter chills with whiskey and "other strong waters" served at a bar hollowed into its side.

Montmorency's awesome falls (*right*), a sheer wall of water with a drop of more than 80 metres. The falls are the highest in eastern Canada.

Just 16 kilometres east of Québec City, the Rivière Montmorency thunders over the edge of an 83-metre-high cliff—a drop 30 metres greater than that of Niagara. This magnificent, silvery curtain of falling water extends about 80 metres at its widest.

Samuel de Champlain discovered the falls in 1603 and named them in honor of Charles de Montmorency, viceroy of New France. The falls themselves, formed several million years earlier, are the result of a prehistoric geological upheaval and the gradual erosion that followed. Fossils of marine life dating back some 11,000 years, to when this area was covered by the Champlain sea, have been discovered along the cliff.

Visitors will find picture-perfect vantage points on the Ile d'Orléans suspension bridge as well as at the top of the falls. There are picnic and observation areas at both the base and summit of the cataract, and several fine walking trails that ramble over the clifftops.

Breathtaking during summer, the falls are transformed into a shimmering wonderland during winter. Mist and spray crystallize as they hit the frigid air, coating the surrounding landscape in a thick glaze and settling in a cone shape at the base of the falls. This frozen peak, nicknamed the "sugarloaf," reaches heights of up to 30 metres. Tobogganers of all ages swarm up it to schuss down its icy slopes.

Tourists for centuries have been drawn to the natural beauty of Montmorency Falls. Sir Frederick Haldimand, Canada's Governor-General from 1778 to 1786, so loved the area that he commissioned Kent House (also known as Maison Montmorency) to be built nearby. This handsome property is now owned and maintained by the provincial government. The building is open to the public.

The 'Niagara' of Québec

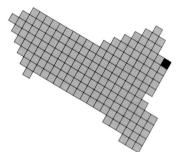

ILE D'ORLEANS

A typical Ile d'Orléans scene (*above*). Farming here is practised much as in the time of the original settlers, some three centuries ago.

The essence of fertility (*right*), Ile d'Orléans is renowned for its tasty, fresh strawberries. When the island was first discovered by Jacques Cartier, however, wild grapes were the fruits most in evidence. He named the island Bacchus, for the Roman god of wine, then later renamed it in honor of the Duke of Orléans, son of Francis I.

Pages 194-195: Mare and foal enjoying the rites of spring on the outskirts of Ste-Pétronille, a small community on the western tip of Ile d'Orléans.

Old-world charm pervades Ile d'Orléans, and visitors can quickly appreciate why the island has been declared a historic region. Anchored just off the shores of Québec City, it stands as a triumphant survivor of French-Canadian rural life in the 1700s, a realm of venerable churches and houses, and weathered farms and barns.

Thirty-five kilometres long and eight kilometres wide, the island supports a variety of agriculture. Potatoes and other vegetables are grown on long narrow farms extending to the river, much as in the time of the original settlers. Orchards yield plums and apples. The island is also noted for its fine strawberries.

On the north side of Ile d'Orléans, where elevation is highest, the land thrusts upward to form lofty cliffs. The channel here harbors a number of species of migratory birds.

A 65-kilometre-long loop road encircles the island, keeping within constant sight of the river and cutting through forests, meadows, and farmlands, to link Ile d'Orléans' six villages. The oldest of these, St-Laurent, dates to 1635.

Each of the six parishes possesses its own distinct character, yet there are similarities in the architecture. All of the island's small, brick-fronted dwellings were built by local mariners in a distinctive design that sets them apart from the houses usually found in rural Québec.

One of the island's best vantage points is on the outskirts of the village of St-Jean. Here the road climbs toward a central plateau, to a panorama of the old-style agricultural landscape and surrounding river.

In 1935, Ile d'Orléans emerged from isolation with the construction of a bridge connecting it to the north shore of the St. Lawrence. But the island has retained its Eden-like simplicity—preserving old ways in tribute to a treasured past.

Island Eden in the St. Lawrence

QUEBEC, LA MAURICIE,
BOIS-FRANCS

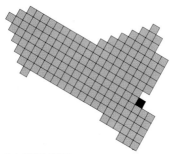

LA PERADE

An instant village (*right*):
fishing shacks on the frozen
Rivière Ste-Anne at La Pérade.
Throughout a two-month
festival here, prizes are awarded
for the best catch and for the
best-decorated cabin.

La Pérade, on the banks of the Rivière Ste-Anne, is one of Québec's most popular ice-fishing spots. In fact, locals have turned the sport into an annual celebration. Toward the end of December, when the ice has frozen to a sturdy thickness and the river beneath is teeming with migrating tommycod, hundreds of box-like cabins pop up across the estuary of the Rivière Ste-Anne. The ice is soon riddled with fishing holes, and for the next two months or so the atmosphere is one of great festivity.

The tiny plywood fishing shelters are equipped with stoves and electricity, as well as with ice-cutting tools, bait, and tackle. Loudspeakers pipe music for the fishermen to sing along with and dance to, and the revelry lasts late into the night. To stir up a little friendly competition, contests are held and prizes awarded for the longest fish caught. The average daily catch is 45 fish. A Mr. Tommycod and festival queen and princesses are chosen to preside over the celebration.

La Pérade lies just 38 kilometres east of Trois-Rivières, and is reached by Route 138, Québec's north shore coastal highway. The village was founded in 1693 under the name of Ste-Anne. Many habitant homes from that period can be seen today, including the well-preserved Gouin (1669), Tremblay (1669), Dorion (1719), and Baribeau (1717) houses.

In 1706 Pierre-Thomas de Lanaudière, seigneur of La Pérade, married Marie-Madeleine de Verchères—Québec's young heroine from the village of the same name. (It is said that when she was 14 she defended her father's seigneurial fort against an Iroquois attack.) When she died in 1747 she was buried in the village church. This church was demolished by fire 28 years later and Madeleine's remains were removed to an unmarked grave. Today a beautiful twin-spired wooden chapel replaces the former structure.

A Fishermen's Festival

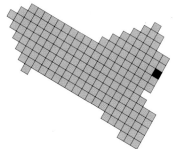

THE PLAINS OF ABRAHAM

The blue St. Lawrence (*above*), as it skirts Québec City. On the far right of the photograph, the green fringes of the Plains of Abraham can be seen.

The Plains of Abraham (*right*), from another angle—once a place where history was made, now a year-round playground. During the 10-day Québec *Carnaval*—in January or February—much of this area is alive with colorful throngs of winter celebrants.

The Plains of Abraham is the best known and probably the most frequented site in Québec City. It is a vast, loosely wooded terrain covering nearly 95 hectares, and is comparable to London's Hyde Park or the Bois de Boulogne in Paris. Forming part of what is known as National Battlefields Park, it was the scene—nearly 225 years ago—of a ten-minute battle that marked the end of the French regime in North America, and set the course of Canadian history.

In the early light of September 13, 1759, British troops under Gen. James Wolfe scaled the cliffs leading up to the Plains and caught the French military off guard. A brief but bloody encounter followed. When it ended, more than 1,200 soldiers lay dead or wounded. The casualties included both Wolfe and the French leader, the Marquis de Montcalm.

At the time of the conquest this historic area was little more than pasture land. It was named the Plains of Abraham after the first owner, Abraham Martin, who grazed cattle here until his death in 1664. The land was then sold to Ursuline nuns who later conceded it to the federal government. The area today has been transformed into a lovely parkland with shady lanes, flower beds, green lawns, and several lookouts offering panoramic views of the city and the narrowing St. Lawrence River.

Eighteen bronze plaques placed throughout the Plains commemorate various battle incidents and the soldiers who took part. Two of these plaques indicate the exact spots where Wolfe and Montcalm fell. There are also several monuments in the park, as well as a fountain and bandstand. Joggers run along the boardwalk, families picnic on the grass, and in the winter these ancient battlegrounds are crisscrossed by skiers and snowshoers.

Battle Site Turned Parkland

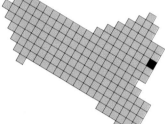

CHATEAU FRONTENAC

Springtime in Québec City
(*above*). In the background, the
familiar outline of the Château
Frontenac.

The Maison Chevalier (*right*), a
restored mansion at the foot of
the Château Frontenac that is
now a museum of early French-
Canadian furniture. The
building dates to 1725.

Château Frontenac's green copper gables and turreted peaks
rise dramatically above the Québec City skyline, forming a
silhouette that over the years has become the symbolic
"ambassador" of this old-world metropolis. The Château's
baronial red brick and distinctive Victorian architecture are
as recognizable a part of Québec as the Arc de Triomphe is of
Paris, or the Empire State Building of New York.

This grand hotel, perched majestically atop Cape Diamond,
plays host to tens of thousands of foreign and domestic visitors
each year. Famous guests have ranged from Winston Churchill
to Charles de Gaulle and Franklin D. Roosevelt.

The building stands on what was once the site of Château
Saint-Louis—the residence of the governors of New France.
(When the Château Saint-Louis was destroyed by fire in 1834,
the official residence was then transferred to nearby Château
Haldimand.) The first of four hotels constructed by the
Canadian Pacific Railway, the Château Frontenac was built
over a two-year period (1893-95). Today, although the interior
of the hotel has been entirely modernized, an air of Victorian
opulence has been preserved.

Next to the Château, in Place d'Armes, calèches await
weary strollers. Dufferin Terrace, a cliff-edge boardwalk graced
with ornate pagodas, stretches from Place d'Armes to the
Citadel, where it connects with another boardwalk called the
Governor's Promenade. This terrace continues along a clifftop
overlooking the St. Lawrence some 70 metres below, and
merges into National Battlefields Park. Lord Durham began
working on the design of these scenic boardwalks around 1838.
Since then, the wooden planks have been well trodden by
generations of lovers and sightseers meandering across from
the Château to the Plains of Abraham.

An Air of Victorian Opulence

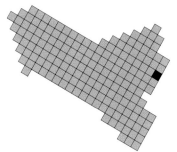

PLACE ROYALE

Two aspects of a window (*above* and *right*) in historic Place Royale. The square today, popular with residents and tourists of all ages, is a far cry from the primitive site where Champlain cleared trees for his Habitation in 1608. At the rear of the square stands Notre-Dame-des-Victoires, a treasure house of exquisite sculptures and wood carvings, and paintings by Rubens and other masters.

Québec City's colonial past has been smartly resurrected in Place Royale, the heart of Lower Town's old port area. Since 1970, when the Québec government assumed trusteeship, this historic district has undergone a splendid renaissance of rebuilding, with many houses now restored to their traditional 18th-century appearance. The area itself is a mere stone's throw from the ferry to Lévis; the Québec Seminary; and the Château Frontenac.

Given its favorable location on the doorstep of maritime trade routes linking New France with the West Indies and the mother country, Place Royale became the colony's commercial hub. Upper Town, on the other hand, emerged as the religious and administrative center.

The English conquest of 1759 brought renewed zeal to business activity in Place Royale. From about 1880 onward, an influx of banks, insurance companies, and law offices displaced many local residents from their homes. These residents gradually relocated along the banks of the Rivière St-Charles and to the neighborhoods of St-Roch, St-Sauveur and St-Jean-Baptiste. The reigning commercial barons had no incentive to preserve deteriorating colonial buildings; instead they erected new ones, often on top of valuable ruins.

After painstaking research and excavation, much of Place Royale has been faithfully restored. The most impressive buildings are those surrounding Notre-Dame-des-Victoires Church (1688), the focal point of the square and still one of the old capital's most popular attractions.

Many of the restored houses have been converted into apartments, boutiques, artists' workshops and restaurants. Several other houses have been transformed into museums. The Maison Soumandre is a reception and information center as well as the departure point for guided tours of the area.

Where History Stands Proud

Even if you are unfamiliar with the French language, the place names and proper names in this book should present no difficulty. Many of the terms used are easily recognizable—a *parc*, for example, is a park, a *baie* is a bay, and a *rivière* is a river. Below is a listing of some other words that appear in the book, along with a contextual translation.

Ami: Friend
Ange gardien:
    Guardian angel
Anse: Cove
Armes: Weapons
Aurore: Dawn

Banc: Bank, embankment
Beau: Good-looking
Beau-fils: Son-in-law
Blanc: White
Bois: Woods
Bon(ne): Good
Bonaventure:
    "Successful adventure"

Calèche:
    Horse-drawn carriage
Canard: Duck
Cap: Cape
Chemin: Path, trail
Coin: Corner

Deux: Two
Diable: Devil
Dieu: God

Eboulement: Landslide
Ecorce: Bark (of tree)
Etang: Pond

Fée: Fairy

Grand(e): Big, great
Gros(se): Big, large
Grue: Crane (the bird)

Havre: Harbor
Hôtel: Hotel, town hall,
    city hall
Hôtel-Dieu: Hospital

Ile: Island
Intendant: Governor
Isle: Island (Old French)

Lac: Lake
Loup: Wolf

Maison: House
Mer: Sea
Meule: Grindstone
Mont: Mount
Montagne: Mountain
Moulin: Mill

Neige: Snow
Nord: North
Notre-Dame: Our Lady
Nouveau: New

Oie: Goose

Percé: Pierced
Père: Father
Pic: Peak
Place: Place, square,
    marketplace
Pleureuse: Tearful
Pointe: Point
Port: Port
Promenade: Walkway

Réserve faunique:
    Wildlife reserve
Renommée: Renowned
Rive: Riverbank
Roche: Rock
Rosier: Rosebush
Rouge: Red
Roy: King (Old French)
Rue: Street

Saumon: Salmon
Sept: Seven

Tourmente: Storm

Vert(e): Green
Victoire: Victory
Ville: Town

Glossary

Index

PICTURE CREDITS

Mia and Klaus: all photographs, with the exception
of those that appear on the following pages
34–35, Maxime St-Amour
38–43, Maxime St-Amour
48, © Michel Gascon/Réflexion
74, Le Centre d'Arts d'Orford JMC
86, Val Mitrofanow
87, Pierre Léveillé
88, Val Mitrofanow
89, Pierre Léveillé
93, Val Mitrofanow
120, Tourisme De Lanaudière
121, Direction générale du Tourisme-Québec
124, Pierre Gaudard
125–131, Centre de documentation, Société d'aménagement de l'Outaouais
134–135, Jacques Lavigne
160, Marc Ellefsen
161, © Anne Gardon/Réflexion
170, Québec, M.L.C.P./Pierre Pouliot
178, Pierre Gaudard
180, Direction générale du Tourisme-Québec
182, Direction générale du Tourisme-Québec

Typesetting: Reader's Digest Typesetting Services
Photolithography and Printing: Herzig Somerville Limited
Binding: Harpell's Press Co-operative
Binding material: Narragansett Coated Paper Corp.
Paper: Hallein Papier AG

The main text of this book has been typeset in 14-point Torino.